W9-AZZ-278

CANAL HOUSE
COOKING

Copyright © 2009 by Christopher Hirsheimer & Melissa Hamilton
Photographs copyright © 2009 by Christopher Hirsheimer
Illustrations copyright © 2009 by Melissa Hamilton

All rights reserved. No part of this book may be reproduced or transmitted in any man-
ner whatsoever without written permission from the publisher, except in the case of
brief quotations embodied in critical articles or reviews.

Canal House
No. 6 Coryell Street
Lambertville, NJ 08530
thecanalhouse.com

ISBN 978-0-692-00317-6

Printed in the United States of America
10 9 8 7 6 5 4 3 2

Book design by Canal House, a group of artists who collaborate on design projects.
This book was designed by Melissa Hamilton, Christopher Hirsheimer & Teresa Hopkins.
Authors' photo by Teresa Hopkins.
Edited by Margo True.
Copyedited by Valerie Saint-Rossy.

CANAL HOUSE
COOKING

Volume N° 1

Hamilton & Hirsheimer

OUR BOOKS

This book launches the publication of our recipe collections—Canal House Cooking. We'll publish three seasonal volumes a year: Summer, Fall & Holiday, and Winter & Spring, each filled with delicious recipes for you from us. To sign up for a subscription or to buy books, visit thecanalhouse.com.

OUR WEBSITE

Our website, thecanalhouse.com, a companion to this book, offers our readers ways to get the best from supermarkets (what and how to buy, how to store it, cook it, and serve it). We'll tell you why a certain cut of meat works for a particular recipe, which boxes, cans, bottles, or tins are worthwhile, which apples are best for baking, and what to look for when buying olive oil, salt, or butter. We'll also suggest what's worth seeking out from specialty stores or mail-order sources and why. And wait, there's more. We will share our stories, the wines we are drinking, gardening tips, events, and our favorite books, cooks, and restaurants—they all will be on our site.

Table of Contents

Grilling in the fireplace at Canal House on a rainy summer day

CANAL HOUSE
COOKING

Welcome to the Canal House—our studio, workshop, dining room, office, kitchen, lair, lab, and atelier devoted to good ideas and good work relating to the world of food. We write, photograph, design, and paint, but in our hearts we both think of ourselves as cooks first.

How did we get here? Neither of us set out to make careers in the food world. Actually there wasn't much of a "foodie" world when we both started. But our deep interests led us down paths that unfolded in front of us.

We had worked with each other as food editors in the magazine world. We traveled the globe in search of essential and authentic recipes, sliding into banquettes in famous restaurants, meeting big deal chefs, and even cooking in far-flung home kitchens. It was great and exciting. But our work took us both away from our families, our homes, and our gardens, away from what really matters, after all.

We live in little towns across the river from each other, one in New Jersey, the other in Pennsylvania. So we decided to join forces. We share similar backgrounds, having grown up in big families where food came first. In a time that seems like a million years ago now, our aproned grandmothers nurtured us with wholesome, comforting food—buttermilk pancakes drenched in salty butter and maple syrup. Our mothers were glamorous. They loved parties and cocktails and restaurants and brunch with Bloody

Marys—food was exciting. Last night's Chinese "takeout" would show up at breakfast reheated with two poached eggs on top. Both of us have deep food memories and large legacies to uphold.

We found our loft studio in an old redbrick warehouse downriver from where we live. A beautiful lazy canal runs alongside the building. One hundred years ago, mules plodding along the tow path hauled provision-ladened barges up and down the state. In warm weather, we throw open the French doors and the voices of the people walking or fishing below float up to us. We plant herbs in our window boxes and grow tomatoes in pots on our wrought-iron balcony. In the winter we build fires in the Franklin wood stove to keep cozy when its snowy and gray outside.

The Canal House has a simple galley kitchen. Two small "apartment-size" stoves sit snugly side by side against a white tiled wall. An old wooden carpenter's worktable with a little sink at one end is our long counter and pots hang from a rack suspended above it. We have a dishwasher, but we find ourselves preferring to hand wash the dishes so we can look out of the tall window next to the sink and see the ducks swimming in the canal or watch the raindrops splashing into the water.

The town around us is a small American river town. A noon whistle still blows and church bells chime—no kidding! There is a drug store around the corner. Across the street is an old hardware store, and the best bar in the world is right down the alley.

And every day we cook. Starting the morning with coffee or cups of sweet milky tea, we tell each other what we made for dinner the night before. In the middle of the day we stop our work, set the table simply with paper napkins, and have lunch. We cook seasonally because that's what makes sense. We want stews and braises and rich thick soups in February when it's snowing and blowing. In mid-summer, we buy boxes of tomatoes to dress as minimally as we do in the heat. And in the height of the season, we preserve all that we can, so as to save a taste of summer.

So it came naturally to write down what we cook. The recipes in this book are what we make for ourselves all summer long. If you cook your way through a few, you'll see that who we are comes right through in these pages: that we are crazy for melons in late summer, that we love to cook big paellas outdoors over a fire for a crowd of friends, that we make jarfuls of teriyaki sauce for slathering on roasted chicken, and tubs of homemade ice cream for our families.

Canal House Cooking Volume N°1 is our first effort. It is a collection of our favorite summer recipes—home cooking by home cooks for home cooks. With a few exceptions, we use ingredients that are readily available and found in most markets in most towns throughout the United States. All the recipes are easy to prepare (some of them a bit more involved), all completely doable for the novice and experienced cook alike. We want to share with you as fellow cooks, our love of food and all its rituals. The everyday practice of simple cooking and the enjoyment of eating are two of the greatest pleasures in life.

Christopher & Melissa

IT'S ALWAYS FIVE O'CLOCK SOMEWHERE . . .

THE SIDECAR
makes 2

The Boat House is the little bar down the alley from us. We call it "the best bar in the world"—because it's there that Christine or Rich whip up side-cars extraordinaire. Our fantasy is that someday one of these expert bar-tenders will climb our stairs and knock on our door at precisely five o'clock with two of these delicious cocktails.

1 lemon

Superfine sugar

3 ounces cognac

1 ounce Cointreau (or Triple Sec)

2 lemon slices

Juice the lemon, reserving the rinds. Rub the rims of two stemmed cocktail glasses with the pulp side of the lemon rind to moisten the rims, then dip the moistened rims into a saucer holding the sugar.

Fill a cocktail shaker with ice. Add the lemon juice, cognac, and Cointreau and shake well. Strain into the sugar-rimmed glasses and garnish each with a slice of lemon.

VARIATION: Change the cognac to Armagnac and you'll be sipping an "Armored Car".

CAIPIRINHA
makes 1

The Caipirinha is Brazil's national cocktail. It looks like a margarita, but it tastes like an intense mojito.

Muddle 1 cut-up lime and 1–2 tablespoons sugar together in a sturdy glass. Add 1 ounce cachaça (sugarcane brandy), fill the glass with ice, and stir well. Drink responsibly; this can knock you on your can as you knock it back.

VARIATION: Substitute vodka for the fiery Brazilian cachaça and you'll be drinking a Caipiroska.

PIMM'S CUP
makes 1

The British drink this refreshing gin-based cocktail when the going gets hot—it's a favorite at sporting events like Wimbledon. At 50 proof, it's civilized enough for you to sip a few before dinner and still find your way to the table. If, on the other hand, you like your cocktail with a bit more punch, substitute 1 ounce of Pimm's No. 1 with gin.

Fill a highball glass with ice. Pour in 2 ounces Pimm's No. 1 and top off with ginger ale. Garnish with 1 cucumber spear or wedge of lime.

PARRISH HOUSE SPECIAL
makes 1 refreshing drink

This is a great aperitif for our nondrinking friends or for us when we are feeling very virtuous. Bitters were developed to stimulate the appetite, aid in digestion, and promote one's general well-being. Of course, the secondary gain is that this is one of the most delicious drinks around. The bitters add an exotic taste.

Squeeze the juice of a fat lime wedge into a tall glass; rub the wedge around the lip of the glass. Shake in about 6 drops Angostura Bitters. Add lots of ice cubes and toss in the lime. Fill two-thirds of the glass with sparkling water and top off with ginger ale.

"SUN" TEA
makes 1 quart

Actually, you don't need the sun to shine to make this old-fashioned, refreshing drink. Brew this a bit strong (the cold-water brewing will keep it from getting bitter) as ice will water it down.

Fill a pitcher or quart jar with cold water and add 6–8 tea bags of your favorite tea. We like good old English Breakfast tea, though Constant Comment is delicious too. Cover and allow the tea to steep in your refrigerator for 4 hours. Remove the tea bags and store covered in the fridge for up to a week (though it will never last that long). Sweeten with Simple Syrup (see next recipe) and drink over lots of ice.

SIMPLE SYRUP
makes 2 cups

We use this syrup to sweeten iced tea, drizzle it over pound cake to moisten and flavor the crumb, spoon it over fresh berries or sliced stone fruit, and add to fruit purées when making sorbets. As long as you remember the formula—2 parts sugar to 1 part water—you can make as much or as little as you like.

Put 2 cups sugar and 1 cup water into a heavy-bottomed saucepan. Heat over medium-low heat, gently swirling the pan over the heat to help dissolve the sugar as it melts.

When the syrup comes to a boil, cover the pan to let the steam run down the sides, washing away and dissolving any sugar granules on the side of the pan, and cook for 2–3 minutes. Let the syrup cool to room temperature. Store in an airtight container in the refrigerator for up to 6 months.

FLAVOR VARIATIONS: Add one of the following to the hot syrup just after it has finished cooking. Once the syrup has cooled, strain it before storing:

2 branches fresh mint, tarragon; basil, rosemary, thyme, or lemon verbena

4 whole star anise

2 teaspoons fennel seeds

1 split vanilla bean

Strips of zest of 1 lemon, orange, lime, or grapefruit

CRÈME DE CASSIS AND CLUB SODA

Christopher always manages to stash some special delicious thing she's found on a trip into her suitcase to share with or give to her friends back home. On one occasion, just back from Burgundy in the heart of France, she pulled out a beautiful bottle with a long slim neck, the cork sealed with red wax. She set out two pretty, tiny glasses, broke open the wax seal, and poured us dainty shots of crème de cassis. We sipped the sweet black currant liqueur, chasing it with cold, bubbly club soda. A perfect way to sip the afternoon away.

On nonsipping days when we have a taste for crème de cassis, we like to fill a short glass with ice, add a good splash of crème de cassis, and top it off with cold club soda.

MELON WATER

Consider the melon: a big juicy orb of sweet, perfumed rainwater. Cookbook author Niloufer Ichaporia King turned us on to yellow watermelon (but any variety or combination of melons will do). Make sure that you work over a bowl to catch every drop. If you are using a watermelon, you might want to save the rind for Watermelon Pickle (page 116).

Crack open a ripe melon. Scrape or pick out the seeds and cut off the rind. Put the chunks of melon and any accumulated juices into a blender and purée until smooth. Strain the purée through a sieve into a pitcher, pushing the juice through with a rubber spatula. Discard the pulp. Add some Simple Syrup (page 9) to sweeten it, if you like.

Serve the melon water in a glass over ice with a big squeeze of lime, a big sprig of mint, and a shot of white rum (though the drink is perfectly delicious without out the rum as well).

HOW TO BOIL AN EGG

Very fresh eggs don't peel well no matter how gently you've boiled them or for how long. The shell clings to the white like a second skin and won't let go without pockmarking it. The remedy is to hang on to your very fresh eggs for about a week in the refrigerator before hard-boiling them. The shell will peel off like a glove. Here's how we hard-boil our eggs so the yolks are pleasantly moist—not crumbly dry—and remain vibrantly yellow with no green-gray ring.

Submerge large eggs straight from the fridge into a pot of gently boiling water (the water should cover the eggs by about 1 inch) and cook for:

6 minutes — the perfect soft-boiled egg

9 minutes — a soft yolk hard-boiled egg

10 minutes — the perfect hard-boiled egg

11 minutes — the firm yolk hard-boiled egg

Drain the eggs in the sink and immediately run cold water into the pot to cool off the eggs. Drain the eggs when they are cool to the touch. They are ready for peeling. Tap the eggs all over on the kitchen counter, then peel off the shell starting from the fatter end of the egg (where the air sac is). Keep the uncracked unpeeled hard-boiled eggs in the refrigerator if you are not going to use them within 4 hours.

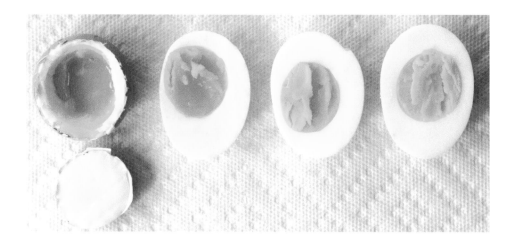

"BUTTERED" EGGS

Sometimes when we are too busy to make deviled eggs, we do something just as good. We simply "butter" the cut sides of hard-boiled eggs with mayonnaise, arrange the eggs on a plate, and drizzle them with some good olive oil and a generous sprinkle of salt and pepper. We often garnish them with something: chopped Preserved Lemon rind (page 120), or chives, or sometimes parsley, tarragon, or dill, or bacon, thinly sliced ham, or chutney. These eggs are delicious and one of our favorite things to eat.

DEVILED EGGS
makes 12

These deviled eggs stand on their own but we often embellish the tops with a dab of harissa (Tunisian chile-spice paste), a fat cooked asparagus tip, shards of crisp bacon, chopped ham, prosciutto, a small spoonful of salmon roe, or a thin slice of cornichon.

6 hard-boiled eggs, peeled

½ cup mayonnaise

1 tablespoon sour cream

1 teaspoon Dijon mustard

Salt and pepper

Cut the hard-boiled eggs in half lengthwise. Pop the yolks out from the whites into a fine sieve set over a bowl. Set the whites aside. Use a wooden spoon to press the yolks through the sieve. Fold in the mayonnaise, sour cream, and mustard. Season with salt and pepper.

Use two teaspoons to fill each egg white with the egg yolks. Garnish the eggs, as you like, (see the headnote) even if it's with just a dash of pimentón, a parsley leaf, or a scattering of finely chopped fresh chives.

Overleaf: Toasts with toppings, top row, left to right: Caramelized Onions, Eggs & Bacon,
Tomato with Anchovy; middle and bottom rows, random order: Chicken Livers with Scallions,
Smoked Salmon with Preserved Lemon rind, Serrano Ham with a Squeeze of Lemon, and
Sardines with Preserved Lemon

LITTLE TOASTS

Small, crispy toasts are the perfect vehicle to transport all the recipes below into your waiting mouth! They very nicely soak up the flavorful juices of their toppings. We use baguettes or any good bread sliced into small rounds or shapes. Arrange the bread on a baking sheet, brush with a good olive oil and toast in a hot oven (400°), turning once until they have browned on both sides. We make lots and store them in tins or plastic bags. They keep well if it's not too humid.

CARAMELIZED ONIONS
makes enough for 8–12 toasts

An inexpensive kitchen staple, the onion, cooked this way turns savory sweet, and jamlike. Accent the sweetness with a salty anchovy on top.

Melt 4 tablespoons butter in a skillet over medium heat. Add 1 large sliced sweet or Spanish onion and cook until golden on the edges, about 10 minutes. Reduce the heat and cook until the onions are very soft and almost jammy, about 45 minutes. Season with salt and pepper. Pile a spoonful of the warm or cooled onions on toast and top with a piece of anchovy.

CANNED SARDINES ON TOAST

We like delicate Norwegian Brislings packed in olive oil. Spread some soft salted butter on toasts or crackers. Lay a sardine on top of each piece of buttered toast or cracker and sprinkle with minced Preserved Lemon rind, (page 120).

CHICKEN LIVERS WITH SCALLIONS
makes enough for 8–12 toasts

We buy whole chickens to cut up ourselves, and save the livers one by one, storing them in a plastic tub in the freezer until we have enough to make this recipe. Sometimes we can't wait so we sauté a fresh one, eating it on a little piece of toast—a cook's treat—while cooking the rest of the chicken.

Sauté chicken livers quickly over lively heat, and avoid crowding the skillet. They should be crispy on the outside and slightly pink on the inside.

3 tablespoons butter

1 tablespoon olive oil

4–6 chicken livers, separated into lobes

2 tablespoons flour

Salt and pepper

4 scallions, coarsely chopped

1 tablespoon sherry

Melt 2 tablespoons of the butter with the olive oil in a skillet over medium-high heat. Dust the livers with the flour, shaking off any excess, and season with salt and pepper. Sauté the livers in the skillet, browning them on one side, for about 2 minutes. Turn them over, and cook for 1 more minute, then remove from the skillet to a plate. Add the scallions, sherry, and the remaining tablespoon of butter to the skillet and cook, swirling the skillet over the heat, until the butter has melted and the scallions are soft, about 1 minute. Season with salt and pepper and serve the livers, topped with the scallions and sauce, on toasts.

EGGS & BACON ON LITTLE TOASTS
makes 8 toasts

These are most delicious when you use eggs that have just been hard-boiled and are still a little bit warm.

8 small pieces of toast

Mayonnaise

2 hard-boiled eggs (page 14), peeled and quartered

Salt and pepper

2–3 strips cooked bacon, crumbled

3–4 fresh chives, minced

Spread each piece of toast with mayonnaise. Put an egg quarter on each piece of toast. Season with salt and pepper. Put a little dollop of mayonnaise on top of each egg to hold the bacon and chives on top.

JULIA, THE FRY QUEEN

Our friend and colleague Julia Lee (left) has perfected the art of deep-frying. She was the director of the test kitchen at Saveur magazine, so she knows how to nail a recipe. And it doesn't hurt that she is also one of the best natural cooks we know. She's really figured out how to fry. We anointed her the Fry Queen. In her own words, here's how she keeps her crown.

✳ I always use canola, peanut, or corn oil (they have high smoke points of 400°– 450°). I heat the oil gradually until it reaches a temperature of 350°. I fry everything at 350°.

✳ You can use a candy thermometer to check the temperature of the oil. Or do what I do—the Chopstick Test. Dip a wooden chopstick into the hot oil until the tip touches the bottom of the pan and if bubbles form right away around the tip—lots of bubbles, like champagne—start frying!

✳ When you are frying large pieces that can take longer to cook, adjust the heat first up and then down. You want the burner at its highest heat and the oil at 350° when you first put the food into the oil. The oil's temperature will drop, then regain its temperature. As the food cooks, reduce the heat a little if the oil gets too hot. Avoid heating the oil to its smoke point as it will cause it to break down.

✳ If you think the temperature has dipped down, gently agitate the oil with a spatula to keep the temperature up—friction causes heat.

✳ You can re-use the oil. After frying, I drain the oil, cool it, and pour it into a clean pickle jar. You can re-use the oil two or three times.

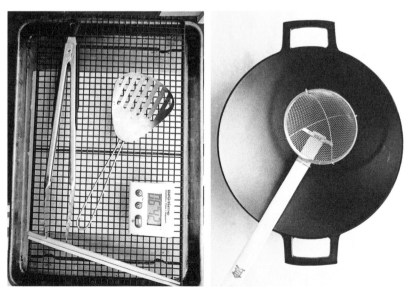

Above left, Julia's frying tools; a small cast iron wok and a spider

FRITTO MISTO
enough batter to serve 6

A fritto misto is a mixed fry—anything, from tiny fish to zucchini blossoms, that has been deep-fried. Our thin all-purpose batter is good for dredging everything from delicate parsley or sage leaves to sturdier slices of lemon, mushrooms, or zucchini batons. The batter should be about the consistency of heavy cream. If it is too thick (flours differ), add a little more wine.

I cup all-purpose flour	Whatever you want to fry, see below
½ teaspoon salt	Canola, peanut, or corn oil
I cup white wine	Salt

For the batter, whisk the flour and salt together in a medium bowl. Gradually add the wine, whisking until the batter is smooth. Give it a quick whisk again just before you're ready to use it.

Prepare whatever you want to fry by cutting it into pieces of uniform or similar shapes and sizes so that things cook at the same rate. Make sure everything is dry, as water/moisture will cause the oil to splatter.

Add enough oil to a heavy skillet or wok to reach a depth of 2 inches. Heat the oil to a temperature of 350°. (See the Fry Queen's tips on page 21.)

Dip whatever you want to fry into the batter, shake off any excess, and carefully lower into the 350° oil. (Be careful not to burn your fingers or splatter the oil!) Fry in small batches turning frequently for even browning. Remove the fritto misto when it is golden or a pale brown. (You'll get the hang of it as you go.) Use a slotted spatula to lift the fritto misto out of the oil and drain on paper towels. Skim any frying debris out of the oil between batches.

Season the fritto misto with salt while it is still hot. Serve as you fry and be sure to keep some for yourself. It's the cooks job to maintain quality control!

FOODS WE LIKE TO DIP & FRY

Fresh sage leaves, fresh parsley sprigs, asparagus, shiitake mushroom caps, zucchini batons or blossoms, Japanese eggplant slices, lemon slices (one of our favorites), scallions, small whole okra, peeled shrimp, small pieces fresh fish . . . you get the idea, it's whatever you want to fry!

TOMATO AND CRAB ASPIC
serves 8

We are partial to Dungeness crab but any lump crabmeat will do. We hold back on the gelatin for a more delicate aspic (the usual ratio is 1 envelope unflavored gelatin to 2 cups of liquid). For a bigger crowd, double the recipe, make it in a large mold or bowl and serve it at the table.

3 cups tomato juice

4 scallions, chopped

I stalk celery, chopped

I small branch fresh tarragon

3 tablespoons fresh lemon juice

Salt

6 black peppercorns

I bay leaf

I envelope unflavored gelatin

I tablespoon sherry

I cup jumbo lump crabmeat, picked over for any stray shells

Parsley leaves for garnish

4 lemon wedges

Put the tomato juice, scallions, celery, tarragon, 2 tablespoons of the lemon juice, 1 teaspoon salt, peppercorns, and bay leaf in a saucepan and simmer over medium-low heat for 20 minutes.

Put ½ cup of cold water into a medium bowl and sprinkle in the gelatin. When the gelatin has softened and swollen, about 5 minutes, strain the hot tomato juice into the bowl with the gelatin, discarding the solids. Stir until the gelatin is completely dissolved.

Add the sherry, the remaining tablespoon of lemon juice, and salt to taste. Stir well.

Divide the crabmeat between eight 8-ounce molds. Pour the aspic over the crabmeat. Cover each mold with plastic wrap and refrigerate until set, about 3 hours or until you are ready to serve.

To unmold the aspic, invert molds onto plates. Wrap the mold in a hot moist dishcloth, reheating the cloth as necessary, until the aspic has softened enough around the edges to slip out of the mold onto the plate. Serve garnished with parsley, lemon wedges, and a simple Bibb leaf salad or with crackers.

MELON AND PROSCIUTTO
serves 4–8, depending on the size of the melon

At the supermarket we pass right by the year-round melons—those ubiqui-tous honeydews and cantaloupes with more texture than flavor. When mel-ons are at the height of their season in late summer at the local farm stands and markets, we can't pass them up, we're like bees drawn to nectar.

Melon has an affinity with salt, and the combination of sweet melon with salty prosciutto is, of course, a well-known Italian classic. My Ameri-can grandfather always ate watermelon—a big wedge of it, using a fork and knife—sprinkled with salt, the shaker next to him on the table so he could re-season as he ate. That was an odd sight to an outdoor-eating, seed-spit-ting, watermelon-for-dessert-minded little kid. —— MH

1 melon (any kind as long as it is ripe and truly in season)
4–8 ounces thinly sliced prosciutto or any dry-cured ham such as
   Serrano, Iberico, or country ham
1 lime, optional

Crack open the melon with a sharp knife and scoop out the seeds with a spoon. Slice the melon into wedges as thick as you like and serve each piece with a few slices of the ham. If you like the tart juice of lime squeezed over the sweetness of the melon and the saltiness of the ham (as we often do), serve a nice chunk of lime on each plate.

SPICED-UP YOGURT SAUCE
makes 1 cup

There are so many delicious yogurts available today, but our favorite is the thick Greek yogurt found in every market.

Mix together in a bowl 1 cup yogurt, the juice of half a lemon, 1 tablespoon honey and a big pinch of ground cardamom. Double or triple the recipe, add more or less of the ingredients to suit your own taste. Serve with a big bowl of ripe summer fruit salad.

SPANISH MUSHROOMS
makes 24

This is one of our favorite tapas. We love its juicy, garlicky flavor. The trick to cooking these mushrooms is to first brown them gill side down, then flip them over to finish cooking so that the little gill cavities fill with delicious mushroom juices. Eat the mushroom first, the toast last, once it's caught all those flavorful juices.

2 cloves garlic
½ bunch parsley, finely chopped
6 tablespoons extra-virgin olive oil
Salt and pepper

24 button mushrooms, stems removed
12 small slices country-style bread
Lemon wedges

Mince 1 garlic clove and mix it with the parsley and 4 tablespoons of the olive oil in a small bowl. Season with salt and pepper and set aside.

Heat the remaining 2 tablespoons of olive oil in a large skillet over medium-high heat. Arrange the mushrooms gill side down in the skillet. Brown the mushrooms without moving them until the bottoms of the caps are golden brown, 2–3 minutes. Turn the mushrooms over. Spoon some of the parsley oil into each mushroom cap. Continue to cook the mushrooms, without moving them, until they are cooked through and their cavities are brimming with juices, 8–10 minutes. Drizzle with a little more olive oil if you like and season with salt and pepper.

While the mushrooms cook, toast the bread slices (see Toast, page 18) then lightly rub the craggy surface of each slice with the remaining garlic clove.

Serve the mushrooms, without spilling any of their precious juices (God forbid!) along with the garlic toasts and lemon wedges.

A BIG BOWL OF SOUP

COLD BORSCHT
(Thanks to Madeleine)
serves 4

In June 1988, a few weeks before we opened my family's restaurant, Hamilton's Grill Room, in Lambertville, New Jersey, my mother, Madeleine, sent me the recipe for this cold soup that she'd found in a soup cookbook, with a note urging me to try it. We opened during a heat wave with no air conditioning and needed a chilled soup. Cold borscht it was—and it remains a summer menu staple there today (twenty-one years later!). —— MH

4 medium beets, trimmed

1 cucumber, peeled, seeded, and diced

Half a small white onion, chopped

1 cup fresh bread crumbs

3 cups sour cream

3 tablespoons Dijon mustard

2 tablespoons heavy cream

¼ cup balsamic vinegar

1 tablespoon sugar

Salt

Minced fresh dill or chives

Preheat the oven to 400°. Wrap each beet in aluminum foil and roast in the oven until tender, about 1 hour. (Take the beets out of the oven, unwrap one, and pierce it with a paring knife to check if it is tender.)

When the beets are cool enough to handle, peel (the skins will slide right off) and dice them. Put the beets into a big bowl. Add the cucumbers, onions, bread crumbs, sour cream (reserve a little for serving, see the picture), mustard, heavy cream, balsamic vinegar, and sugar. Mix well.

Working in batches, purée the beet mixture in a blender until smooth. Use up to ¼ cup water to thin the soup. Season with salt. Transfer to a covered container and allow the flavors to develop in the refrigerator overnight or up to 3 days. This soup improves with time.

Serve the soup in chilled soup bowls or pretty glasses. Garnish with a spoonful of sour cream or a drizzle of heavy cream, and minced fresh dill or chives.

MARIA'S GAZPACHO IN 5 MINUTES
serves 4

When our friend Maria Millán moved back home to Spain recently, we asked her if she'd leave us with her recipe for gazpacho. It's the simplest of versions, with just tomatoes, peppers, and bread pureéd together. We think of it as a working woman's special because it's so quick to make. Here is the recipe just as she wrote it to us:

I use a glass blender. The point is to fill it with tomatoes.

4 or 5 fist-size ripe and peeled tomatoes.* Cut them in thick slices, or however you want, it's just so they fit better in the blender.

One medium-size green pepper (those that you call Italian). It should not be spicy. Seed it and cut it, and add to the blender.

2 cloves of garlic (if you like it garlicky you can put 3, for the kids I stay with 2).

One slice of bread previously soaked in 1 cup of water. Pour the bread with the remaining water into the blender. (I use about 2 inches of baguette, or Italian style, but you can put your regular slice, if it is old, or hard bread better.)

About 2 tablespoons of red wine vinegar, (sherry vinegar, it's fine too, NOT WHITE VINEGAR, PLEASE. Modena [balsamic vinegar] it's OK).

About 3 tablespoons of extra-virgin olive oil.

Salt to taste, about 2 teaspoons (normal salt).

Hit the button, and blend until it is all liquefied. The result should not be too thick/paste-like.**

And that's your gazpacho.

NOTE: If it needs more salt or vinegar, or even garlic, it can be added after it has been blended. It is trickier to add oil.

PS*: I don't always peel them because I don't have a fuzzy [fussy] family. Some of my friends peel them and then after it's blended they put it through the "pasapuré" [foodmill] (I forget how you call that in English, it's an object that has holes on the bottom and a little handle that you turn around several times until the food goes though the holes, so that way the seeds or peel stays behind) I don't think it's at all needed, and it's a new thing with all the delicate people in this modern world.

PPS**: If you put more bread, like double of what I suggested you may get a thicker paste and that is called SALMOREJO, which is also delicious and you serve it sprinkled with very small thin pieces of jamón serrano or jabugo (Half the size of a chocolate chip) and slices of hard-boiled eggs.

Serve cold. You can garnish it with cucumber cut in small cubes (I usually have a bowl and people add if they want it). My grandparents used to put green grapes floating in it, and it was delicious, the contrast is great.

It makes a nice meal with the tortilla de patata, or some chicken/ham, or whatever croquetas or empanadillas, or just plain grilled chicken breast.

One blender could be enough for 4 servings . . . However I usually make 2 blenders because the servings are not dainty when it comes to gazpacho around here.

CONSOMMÉ "MADRILÈNE"
serves 2–3

This refreshing first course was popular in pre–air-conditioned times for ladies' luncheons. Growing up, we always had five or six cans chilling in the back of the fridge. Campbell's actually used to make a consommé madrilène (i.e., in the style of Madrid). Alas, it is gone now. But their standard consommé chills into a cold, clear, soft, amber, intensely flavored jelly—magic on a hot summer day, and it couldn't be simpler "to make". —— CH

Pour a can of Campbell's Consommé into a small saucepan. Add 2–3 tablespoons good sherry and warm over low heat until the jellied soup and sherry just meld together. Pour into a flat dish or bowl and refrigerate until it gels. Scoop the jelled soup into little bowls or wide-mouthed short glasses and garnish with a squeeze of lemon and lots of minced fresh chives.

LAZY MAN'S VARIATION: Keep cans of consommé in your refrigerator and simply scoop the jellied soup from the can into bowls and garnish with a squeeze of lemon and scattering of chives.

TWO WAYS TO MAKE POTATO LEEK SOUP
serves 6

We both love this recipe but we finish it differently. CH usually likes to serve it puréed, hot or cold, depending on the weather and her mood. MH likes the gutsier texture of the crushed soup. Then sometimes we switch. The soup will be gray if you don't trim off the dark green portion leaves of the leeks.

3 tablespoons butter

6 leeks, trimmed, washed, and thickly sliced crosswise

Salt and pepper

6 small russet potatoes, peeled and thickly sliced

6 cups chicken stock

2 bay leaves

Pinch of nutmeg

½ cup thick Greek yogurt

1 cup heavy cream

Fresh chives or chopped parsley

Melt 2 tablespoons of the butter in a large heavy-bottomed pot over medium heat. Add the leeks, season with salt and pepper (you could use white pepper if you prefer), and cook until the leeks have softened, not browned, about 10 minutes. Add the potatoes, chicken stock, bay leaves, and nutmeg. Cover and cook over medium to medium-low heat until the vegetables are soft, 20–30 minutes.

FOR THE PURÉED SOUP

Discard the bay leaves, add the remaining tablespoon of butter, and purée the soup in a blender. Adjust the seasonings. Serve the soup hot or cold garnished with a generous spoonful of yogurt and some chopped chives.

FOR THE CRUSHED SOUP

In the pot, lightly crush the potatoes into pieces using the back of a large spoon. Stir in the cream and adjust the seasonings. Add the remaining tablespoon of butter to the soup. Serve the soup garnished with fresh chives or chopped parsley.

HOW MANY WAYS CAN YOU

USE OLIVE OIL & LEMON ?

CANAL HOUSE SALAD
serves 2–4

When you are in a hurry to get dinner on the table, washing and drying lettuce can seem like "too much trouble". If it keeps you from making salads, do what we do. . .

FOR THE GREENS

Wash lots of young lettuces in a large bowl of cold water, lifting the leaves out of the water and leaving any dirt to settle on the bottom. Do this until there is no more dirt. Shake off any water from the leaves or use a salad spinner. Roll the leaves up in a clean dish towel and store in an open big plastic bag in the refrigerator. Greens can be prepped several days ahead.

FOR THE VINAIGRETTE

Purée 1 small garlic clove and 1 anchovy fillet or a squirt of anchovy paste together in a mortar and pestle. Whisk in the juice of half a lemon and ¼ cup really good extra-virgin olive oil, adding more to suit yourself. Season with salt and pepper. Stir in a handful of minced fresh parsley leaves. (Or you can simply use a heavy knife to chop and mash the anchovy, garlic, and parsley together on a cutting board. Add a little kosher salt to add "grit", which will help the chopping process. Then transfer to a small bowl and whisk in the lemon, oil, and pepper.)

FOR THE SALAD

Pour the vinaigrette into a large salad bowl. Put 4–6 cups of greens on top and bring the whole thing to the table but don't toss until you are ready to serve.

LAZY MAN'S DELICIOUS SALAD VINAIGRETTE
serves 4

Put 4–6 cups of greens in a salad bowl. Squeeze the juice of 1 lemon through your fingers and over the greens, catching and discarding the seeds. Then drizzle some really good extra-virgin olive oil (about ¼ cup) over the greens. Season the salad with coarse salt (Diamond Crystal kosher salt or Maldon Sea Salt are nice) and a few grinds of pepper. Toss the salad and serve.

VINAIGRETTE IN THE BOTTOM OF A SALAD BOWL
(or how French women do it)
serves 4

I small clove garlic
Coarse salt and pepper
I teaspoon Dijon mustard
I tablespoon red wine vinegar or
  fresh lemon juice

3–4 tablespoons really good
  extra-virgin olive oil
4–6 cups salad leaves

Use a wooden spoon to mash together the garlic, salt, and pepper in the bottom of a wooden salad bowl. Stir in the mustard and vinegar. Add the olive oil, stirring as you do so. Taste the vinaigrette and adjust the seasonings. Pile all the salad leaves on top of the vinaigrette. Bring the salad to the table but don't toss it until you're ready to serve.

PRESERVED LEMON VINAIGRETTE
makes enough for salad for 4

Depending on the salty intensity of your preserved lemons, you may or may not want to rinse them. Use only the rind for this vinaigrette.

Rind of half a preserved lemon
  (page 120)
Juice of half a fresh lemon

⅓ cup really good extra-virgin
  olive oil
Salt and pepper

Finely chop the preserved lemon rind and put it into a small bowl or into the bottom of the bowl you're going to use to dress something (greens, potato salad, fresh tomatoes, roasted peppers, sliced cucumbers and celery— you get the idea; you'll see how versatile this vinaigrette is once you've tasted it). Stir in the fresh lemon juice, then the olive oil, and season with pepper. Taste the vinaigrette and add a little salt if you think it needs it.

GREEN GODDESS DRESSING
makes 1½ cups

We use this creamy, very herbaceous dressing on sturdy lettuces like iceberg or romaine, or on wedges of small tight Bibb. We've also been known to spoon some on cold plump peeled shrimp.

¾ cup mayonnaise
⅓ cup sour cream
1 tablespoon white wine vinegar
Half a bunch watercress, leaves
  roughly chopped
6–8 chives, chopped

Quarter bunch parsley, leaves
  roughly chopped
Leaves from 2 large sprigs fresh
  tarragon
4 anchovy fillets
Salt and pepper

Put the mayonnaise, sour cream, vinegar, watercress, chives, parsley, tarragon, and anchovies into a blender or food processor and purée until smooth. Season with a little salt, if the dressing needs it, and a good grinding of black pepper. This dressing will keep, covered, in the refrigerator for up to one week.

CREAMY BLUE CHEESE DRESSING
makes 1¾ cups

We swear this dressing is so delicious we would rather have a big bowl of it than a bowl of ice cream. Use it as a dip for celery or go retro and serve it with potato chips. There is always French Roquefort, but since there are such great American blues right now, try one of those.

½ cup sour cream
½ cup mayonnaise
½ cup buttermilk
2 scallions, finely chopped

½ small clove garlic, minced
½ cup crumbled blue cheese
Salt and pepper

Put the sour cream, mayonnaise, buttermilk, scallions, and garlic into a bowl and stir until well combined. Fold in the blue cheese and season with a little salt, if the dressing needs it, and a good grinding of black pepper. This dressing will keep, covered, in the refrigerator for up to one week.

CORN, STRING BEAN & POTATO SUCCOTASH SALAD
serves 4–6

We'll often make this salad with leftover cooked corn. And if we have a little summer squash or fresh peas or favas on hand, we'll cook them up and add them. You needn't worry if you have a little more of one ingredient or a little less of another—this salad isn't finicky. One more thing about this salad is that from time to time we'll toss in (at the end) some pitted oil-cured olives and small chunks of salty cheese like feta or ricotta salata. Add those, and you've got a meal.

4 thin-skinned waxy potatoes
Salt
4 ears corn, shucked
½ pound string beans, trimmed
I shallot, 2 scallions, or half a small onion (any color is fine), finely chopped

Handful fresh parsley leaves, chopped
⅓ cup really good extra-virgin olive oil
Pepper

Cook the potatoes in a large pot of boiling salted water over medium-high heat. While the potatoes are cooking, add the corn to the pot and cook for 3–5 minutes. Pull the corn from the boiling water and let it cool. Next add the string beans to the pot and cook until tender, about 5 minutes. Scoop the string beans out of the boiling water with a large slotted spoon or a pair of tongs and put them into a bowl of cold water to cool them down quickly. Drain the potatoes when they are tender, about 20 minutes depending on their size.

Cut the corn off the cob into a large bowl. Cut the potatoes into slices or chunks and add them to the bowl with the corn. Drain the beans and put them into the bowl. Add the shallots, parsley, and olive oil, and season with salt and lots of pepper. Toss and adjust the seasonings adding more salt and pepper and some olive oil if the succotash is a little dry.

Overleaf: Corn, String Bean & Potato Succotash Salad

A NICE NIÇOISE FOR NEXT TO NIL
serves 4

This familiar salad sometimes gets overlooked. But it's why we keep good quality canned tuna packed in olive oil (the key to moist and flavorful canned tuna!) in our pantry. Albacore is king—it's high fat, and its pale flesh make it the only canned tuna permitted to be called "white". Equally delicious are *ventresca* (Italian tuna belly) *ventrèche* (in French) and *bonito* (a dark-fleshed tunalike fish from Spain).

4 thin-skinned waxy potatoes

Salt

2 handfuls of string beans,
    preferably skinny haricots verts

4 tomatoes

4–6 anchovy fillets

Pepper

2–3 cans or jars tuna packed
    in olive oil

Half a lemon

2 tablespoons capers

4–6 tablespoons really good
    extra-virgin olive oil

1 head of Bibb lettuce

4 hard-boiled eggs, peeled and
    quartered (page 14)

Handful black oil-cured olives, pitted

Small handful fresh parsley leaves,
    chopped

Cook the potatoes in a large pot of boiling salted water over medium-high heat. While the potatoes are cooking, add the string beans to the pot and cook until tender, about 5 minutes. Scoop the string beans out of the boiling water with a large slotted spoon or a pair of tongs and put them into a bowl of cold water to cool them down quickly. Drain and set them aside.

Blanch the tomatoes in the boiling water very briefly to loosen the skin. Core and peel the tomatoes, slice them into quarters or large chunks, and set them aside.

Test the potatoes with the tip of a sharp knife and when it slides in easily, they are cooked through, about 20 minutes depending on their size. Drain the potatoes, let them cool, then thickly slice them.

Coarsely crush the anchovies and some salt and pepper together in a sturdy little bowl. (If you like its flavor, add some of the oil from the can of tuna.) Squeeze the juice from the lemon into the bowl. Add the capers and stir in the olive oil. Taste the vinaigrette and adjust the seasonings.

Assemble the salad on a big serving platter or on individual plates. Start by arranging the lettuce leaves on the platter, then place the tuna, potatoes, string beans, tomatoes, and hard-boiled eggs around the platter in clusters. Dress the salad with the vinaigrette and garnish it with the olives and chopped parsley.

SHAVED RAW ASPARAGUS WITH LEMON-ANCHOVY VINAIGRETTE
serves 2–4

This really is a nowhere-to-run-nowhere-to-hide recipe. It relies on the brightest and best flavors and crispest textures of the raw vegetables you use. Be careful with the mandoline. It's the perfect tool for the job but it is easy to cut yourself, so use the guard. You can also make the salad with shaved fennel, celery, or radishes.

4–6 anchovy fillets, chopped
I small clove garlic
Salt and pepper
Juice of half a lemon

¼ cup really good extra-virgin olive oil
I bunch asparagus

Put the anchovies, garlic, and a pinch of salt and a good grinding of pepper in a mortar and crush with a pestle to a coarse paste. Stir in the lemon juice and olive oil. Taste the vinaigrette and season with a little more salt if it needs it. (Or you can simply use a heavy knife to chop and mash the anchovies and garlic together on a cutting board. Add a little kosher salt and pepper to add "grit" which will help the chopping process. Transfer to a small bowl and stir in the lemon juice and olive oil.)

Snap off the tough ends of the asparagus, bending the spears with two hands to find the natural snapping point, and discard the ends. Using a mandoline, carefully slice the asparagus lengthwise into long thin ribbons. Toss the asparagus with the vinaigrette in a bowl.

POTATO SALAD "BUTTERED" AND LEMONED
serves 6

Assembling the salad while the potatoes are still warm allows them to absorb the flavors of all the "fixins".

2–3 pounds potatoes, any
   variety will do
Salt
1 cup mayonnaise
½ cup really good extra-virgin
   olive oil

Pepper
Rind from 1 preserved lemon
   (page 120), chopped
Chopped fresh chives or parsley

Peel the potatoes if you use a thick-skinned variety or if you simply prefer peeled potatoes for this dish. Put the potatoes in a large pot of cold water generously seasoned with salt. Bring to a boil over medium-high heat and cook until they are tender. Drain.

When they are cool enough to handle, slice the potatoes and arrange them on a serving platter, "buttering" one side of each slice with some of the mayonnaise as you work. Drizzle the potatoes with the olive oil, season them with salt and pepper, and garnish the potatoes with the preserved lemons and chives.

OLD-FASHIONED POTATO SALAD

We make this old-fashioned–style potato salad in layers. It still tastes familiar and delicious, but "fresher" than your average deli variety. Here is our template. Use whatever ingredients you fancy or follow your family tradition.

Assemble the salad: In a large shallow bowl or a platter layer sliced warm potatoes, salt and pepper, a nice drizzle of really good olive oil, mayonnaise, finely chopped celery, sliced hard-boiled eggs (page 14), chopped scallions or minced red onions, and a little crispy bacon. Then start all over with the layers. Make it as decadent as you wish.

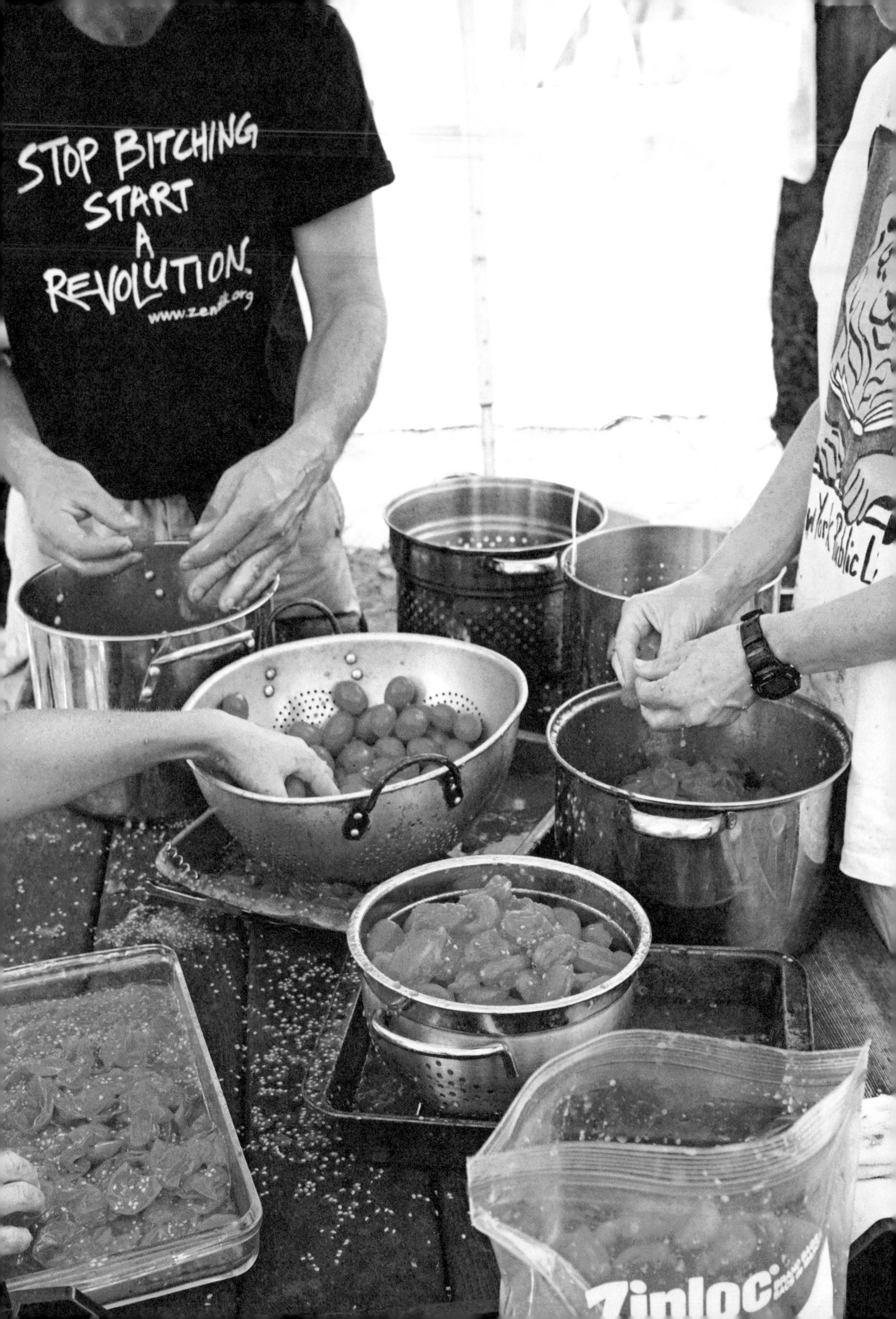
STOP BITCHING
START
A
REVOLUTION.
Ziploc

TOO MANY TOMATOES

BAKED TOMATOES STUFFED WITH RICE
makes 8

Choose summer tomatoes that are ripe and juicy, but not too soft or they will collapse while baking. These tomatoes taste better when eaten at room temperature rather than straight from the oven. The rice, impregnated with the oily tomato juices, has a chance to settle into the meaty tomato, absorbing more flavor as it cools.

8 medium tomatoes, stemmed

6 tablespoons Arborio or other short-grain rice

Handful fresh parsley leaves, finely chopped

2 cloves garlic, minced

6 tablespoons extra-virgin olive oil

Salt and pepper

Preheat the oven to 400°. Slice off the bottom quarter of each tomato (that is, the end opposite from the stem) and set the 8 pieces aside. Working over a large measuring cup to catch all the seeds and juices, use a small spoon to carefully scoop out the interior pulp without piercing the walls of the tomatoes. Arrange the tomatoes cut side up in a baking dish just big enough for them to fit comfortably.

Lift out the large pieces of tomato pulp from the measuring cup and chop finely. Return the chopped pulp to the cup and discard all but 1½ cups of the pulpy liquid. Add the raw rice, parsley, garlic, and 4 tablespoons of the olive oil. Season well with salt and pepper. Fill each tomato with some of the seasoned rice and juices. Place one of the reserved tomato bottoms on top of each filled tomato. Drizzle the remaining 2 tablespoons of olive oil all over the tomatoes.

Bake the tomatoes until the rice is tender and the tomatoes are soft, 40–50 minutes. Let the tomatoes cool to room temperature before serving them.

OVEN-DRIED TOMATOES
makes as many as you want to make

These tomatoes are good to eat warm from the oven and served on top of little toasts (page 18) as an hors d'oeuvre. We like the meaty plum tomato because it's nicely sturdy and holds up to oven-drying and storing, but other varieties of medium-to-small tomatoes work fine, too. When tomatoes are in season, we oven-dry several sheet pans' worth, then store small packets of them in the freezer to use in things like sauces and stews throughout tomato wilderness—the long dark time between locally grown tomato seasons.

Preheat the oven to 325°. Arrange ripe plum tomatoes, halved lengthwise, cut side up on a sheet pan in a single layer. Drizzle them with a little bit of extra-virgin olive oil, then season them with salt and pepper.

Roast the tomatoes in the oven until they've shriveled up a bit and their juices have concentrated and caramelized somewhat, about 1½ hours. (Or let them cook overnight in the oven on it's lowest heat setting. Beware, the aroma may keep you up all night!) Drizzle the tomatoes with a little more oil when they come out of the oven.

If you plan to store some of these tomatoes, pack them into small containers or resealable plastic bags or in food-saver packets with a bay leaf or sprig of fresh rosemary or basil and a bit more olive oil. They keep in the fridge for a week or so, or in the freezer for up to a year.

 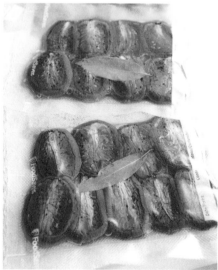

TOMATOES ALL DRESSED UP FOR SUMMER
serves 4–6

The private pleasure of eating a tomato sandwich over the sink with the juices dripping through your fingers and down your chin is one of our constant summer rituals. These tomatoes are so sensual that you might think they should be eaten behind closed doors.

8–12 slices crusty bread

I cloves garlic, peeled

½ cup really good extra-virgin olive oil

4–6 tomatoes, cored and thickly sliced

½ cup mayonnaise

Salt and pepper

Small handful fresh chives, chopped

Small handful of fresh parsley leaves, chopped

Toast the slices of bread. While the toast is still warm, rub one side of each slice with the garlic, rubbing more or less firmly depending on how much flavor you're after. Drizzle the toast with some of the olive oil and sprinkle with some salt.

"Butter" the tomato slices with the mayonnaise and arrange them on a serving platter. Drizzle the tomatoes with the remaining oil, season well with salt and pepper, and scatter the fresh herbs on top. You can place the tomatoes on top of the toasts or just serve the toasts on the side.

TOMATO "ROLLMOPS"

Halve ripe plum tomatoes lengthwise and remove the seeds, leaving just the meaty shells. With the tomatoes cut side up, drizzle with really good extra-virgin olive oil, give a few grinds of pepper, and place half an anchovy fillet and I basil leaf into each tomato half. Stack the filled tomatoes in a container with a lid and add enough olive oil to cover the tomatoes completely. Refrigerate and use in salads, on toasts, or pasta. They will keep for a week. We prize the oil flavored by such deliciousness and use it for everything.

ROASTED TOMATOES STUDDED WITH GARLIC
serves 4

Our friend and great chef and salumi wizard, Paul Bertolli, of Berkeley's Fra' Mani, suggested that we make this for a dinner in honor of esteemed writer Colman Andrews and his wife Erin. We were flying back to New York from California just in time to make the party so Paul wrapped up some of his private stash of garlic and tomatoes, which flew across the country in the overhead compartment. We spun up the recipe a little (the nerve!), but his idea remains central—everyone gets a soft luscious tomato to crush into the nest of pasta.

½ cup diced pancetta

6 tablespoons extra-virgin olive oil, plus more for the pasta

2 anchovy fillets

1 cup coarse fresh bread crumbs

4 tomatoes, tops sliced off, seeds scooped out

2 cloves garlic, thinly sliced

Small handful fresh thyme, parsley, or basil leaves, chopped

Salt and pepper

½ pound spaghetti

Preheat the oven to 350°. Fry the pancetta in a skillet over medium heat until browned and crisp around the edges. Use a slotted spatula to lift the pancetta out of the skillet to a plate. Leave the rendered fat in the skillet. Add 2 tablespoons of the olive oil and the anchovies to the same skillet. Use a wooden spoon to mash the anchovies until they dissolve. Add the bread crumbs and cook, stirring often, until they are golden.

Put the tomatoes, cut side up, in a baking dish and slip some garlic into each tomato. Mound some bread crumbs into each tomato and scatter pancetta and herbs on top. Season with salt and pepper and drizzle the remaining 4 tablespoons of oil over all. Roast the tomatoes in the oven until they have browned a bit and the interior is supple but the tomatoes haven't collapsed, 1–1½ hours.

Cook the spaghetti in a large pot of boiling salted water. Drain. Return the pasta to the pot and stir in some olive oil and some of the oily tomato juices from the bottom of the tomato roasting dish.

Serve the spaghetti with the roasted tomatoes and their juices spooned on top.

STEPHEN'S SUMMER SPAGHETTI
serves 4

Our friend Steven Wagner, who grew up in Rome, is one of the best cooks around. He taught us this recipe about ten years ago, and every summer we make it three times a week in the height of tomato season. The aroma when all that basil hits the oil in the skillet—now that's amore!

1 pound spaghetti
Salt
½ cup olive oil
4 cloves garlic
Great big bunch basil, leaves chopped

6 tomatoes, halved, cored, squeezed of seeds and juice, chopped
Pepper
1 cup freshly grated parmigiano-reggiano

Cook the spaghetti in a large pot of boiling salted water over high heat.

Meanwhile, heat the olive oil in large skillet over medium heat. Add the garlic and cook until it softens and turns a little golden. Remove the garlic and discard. Add all the basil, then the tomatoes, and stir around until just heated through. Season to taste with salt and pepper.

When the pasta is about three-quarters cooked, drain out most of the water, leaving about ½ cup pasta cooking water in the pot. Return the pot with the spaghetti to the heat. Pour in all the tomatoes, oil, and basil lusciousness from the skillet and let it finish cooking for about 5 minutes. Stir in the grated cheese. Serve with a little more olive oil and more cheese.

PLUM TOMATO SAUCE

If tackling a whole case of plum tomatoes is too daunting, then just figure you'll get about 1 cup of tomato sauce for every 10 plum tomatoes. This sauce is plain, pure tomato flavor. It can be used as you might use canned crushed tomatoes.

I case plum tomatoes

4 onions, cut in half through the root end

4 branches fresh rosemary, thyme, oregano, basil, or whatever herb you prefer

Salt and pepper

Cut the tomatoes into halves or quarters and divide them equally, along with their juice, between two large heavy-bottomed stockpots. (Dividing the tomatoes into two [or three if necessary] pots reduces the volume, allowing the sauce to cook more quickly. It is also easier to manage smaller pots.) Add 2 onions and 2 herb branches to each pot and season with salt and pepper. Bring the tomatoes to a boil over medium-high heat, then reduce the heat to maintain a simmer, letting the sauce cook and bubble away until the flesh is totally soft, 2–3 hours. Stir often with a wooden spoon to be sure that it isn't burning on the bottom.

Let the tomatoes cool a bit (an hour or so). Remove the onions (they are good drizzled with olive oil, seasoned with salt and pepper, and baked in a preheated 350° oven until browned on top) or discard them. Pass the tomatoes through a food mill into another large clean pot, discarding the solids.

Cook the tomato sauce over medium heat until the liquid evaporates and the sauce is thick and meaty, 2–3 hours, or until it is as thick as you like. Season with salt. (Or let the sauce cook down overnight in the oven on its lowest heat setting.)

Let it cool completely before dividing it up between lidded containers. The sauce will keep for a week in the refrigerator or up to a year in the freezer.

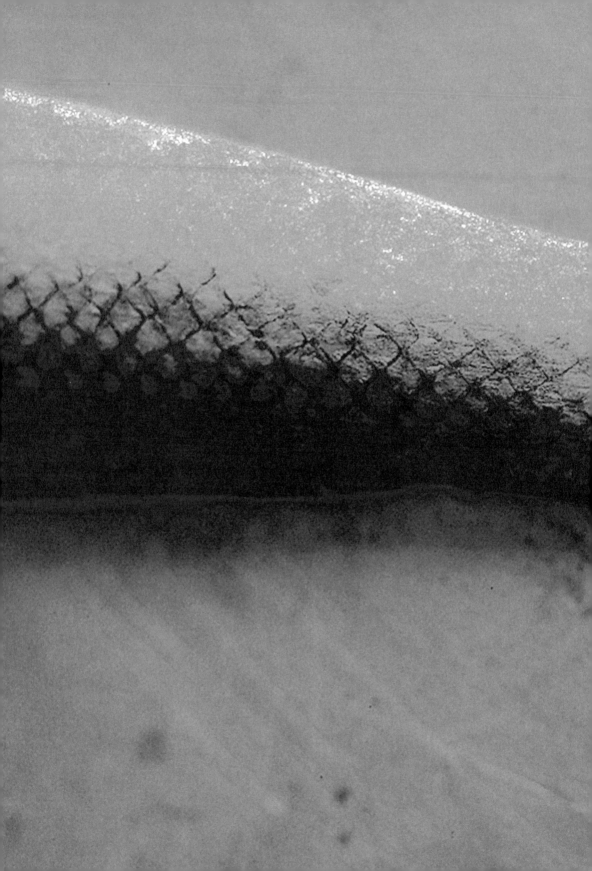

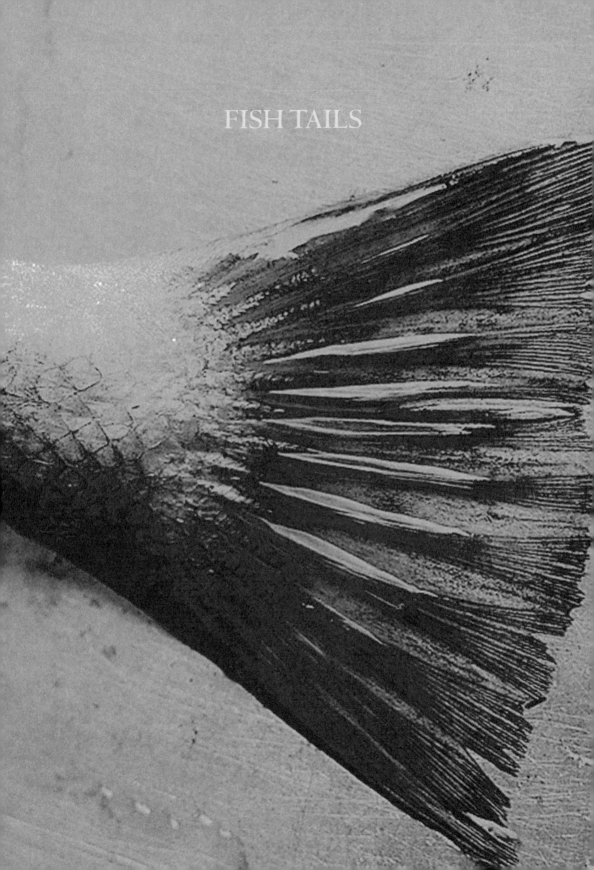

FISH TAILS

COLD LOBSTER WITH HOMEMADE MAYONNAISE
serves 2

We doctor Hellman's mayonnaise with fresh lemon juice, a little minced garlic, and some really good olive oil on occasion, but for a luxurious cold lobster meal, a homemade mayonnaise really is called for. We like to serve bone-cold champagne and hot salty homemade potato chips with the lobsters. If you'd rather not steam your own lobster, ask your fishmonger to do it.

Two 1½-pound live lobsters
1 lemon, halved

FOR THE MAYONNAISE
1 large egg yolk
¼ clove garlic, finely minced (page 84)

Salt
Juice of half a lemon
½ cup canola oil
½ cup good smooth "buttery" olive oil
2 tablespoons finely chopped fresh chervil or tarragon leaves (optional)

Add water to a large pot to a depth of 2–3 inches. Be sure the pot is big enough to accommodate a large colander. Bring the water to a boil over high heat.

Put the lobsters in the colander and place the colander inside the pot. Cover the pot and steam the lobsters for 15 minutes. Remove the colander with the lobsters and allow them to cool. Refrigerate the lobsters until fully chilled, about 2 hours.

For the mayonnaise, whisk together the egg yolk, garlic, a pinch of salt, and half the lemon juice in a medium bowl. Combine the oils in a measuring cup with a spout. Add the oil to the yolk about 1 teaspoon at a time, whisking constantly. The mixture will thicken and emulsify. After you have added about ¼ cup of the oil, you can begin to slowly drizzle in the remaining oil as you continue to whisk until you have a thick, glossy mayonnaise. Season with salt and thin with a little lemon juice if you like. Transfer the mayonnaise into a serving bowl. Cover and refrigerate until ready to use. If using the herbs, stir them into the mayonnaise just before serving.

Put the lobsters on a cutting board, belly side down. Using a large kitchen knife, cut each lobster in half lengthwise. Crack the claws and knuckles with a nutcracker or by thwacking the back of the knife against the shells.

Arrange each lobster on a plate, cut side up, and add a lemon half to each plate. Pass the mayonnaise at the table.

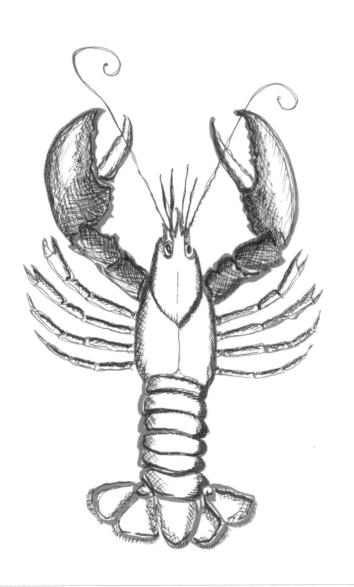

MUSSEL SCALLION STEW
serves 8

You can always find mussels, wherever you go. We see them at our fishmonger and supermarket alike. And it seems that everyone (even little kids) loves the sweet flavor of these pink morsels.

2 onions, chopped

2 teaspoons fennel seeds

1 branch fresh thyme

2 bay leaves

1 teaspoon crushed red pepper flakes

1 bottle white wine

6 pounds mussels, rinsed and debearded

4 tablespoons butter

4 bunches scallions, white and green parts chopped separately

One 28-ounce can whole peeled plum tomatoes

2 cups heavy cream

Put the onions, fennel seeds, thyme, bay leaves, pepper flakes, and wine into a large pot, cover, and simmer over medium-high heat for 10–15 minutes. Add the mussels, cover the pot, and steam them, shaking the pot from time to time, until the shells have opened, about 10 minutes.

Strain the mussels through a fine sieve, catching the broth in a large bowl. Pick the mussels from the shells, putting them into another bowl, and discard the shells and any unopened mussels. Cover the mussels and refrigerate.

Melt the butter in a heavy-bottomed medium pot over medium-low heat. Add the white parts of the scallions and cook until soft, about 5 minutes. Add the tomatoes and any juices from the can into the pot, crushing the tomatoes with your hand as you put them in. Simmer the tomatoes for about 10 minutes.

Add the mussel broth (watch out for any grit in the bottom of the bowl) and the cream to the pot and simmer for 10 minutes. Reduce the heat to medium-low. Add the mussels and the scallion greens and simmer until the mussels are heated through. Ladle into bowls and serve with hot crusty bread.

GRILLED SALMON WITH GREEN OLIVE SAUCE
serves 6–8

For years I followed my mother's lead and turned the grilling over to "the man". It does seem like a guy thing, but like my father before him, my husband would stand outside in the dark smoking and looking at the stars and come in half an hour later with burnt or burnt and raw offerings. So I finally stepped up and took on the grill. One of my favorite things to cook is this grilled salmon. Grilling fish can be a challenge. Its delicate, fragile flesh doesn't tolerate too much handling. My trick here is to lay a whole side of salmon on the grill skin side down. Then I don't touch it until I take it off the grill. The smoke will turn the flesh a pale golden color. —— CH

1 side of salmon
Extra-virgin olive oil
Salt and pepper

FOR THE GREEN OLIVE SAUCE
2 cups pitted green olives such as French green Arnaud or Italian Cerignola, crushed and minced

Rind of 2 preserved lemons (page 120), minced
1 small shallot, finely minced
1 cup parsley leaves, finely chopped
1 anchovy fillet, minced
½ cup really good extra-virgin olive oil
Salt and pepper

Preheat a grill. If you are using a charcoal grill, build your fire to one side of the grill. If using a gas grill, fire up the "back burner". You want heat and smoke but not direct flame, which can incinerate the delicate fish.

Rub the flesh side of the salmon with olive oil and season well with salt and pepper. Lay the fish skin side down on a cookie sheet with no edges. Slide the fish off the cookie sheet onto the grill away from direct flame. Cover with the lid and grill over medium-hot heat until the fish is just cooked through, about 30 minutes. To test if the fish is cooked through, slip the point of a paring knife into the center of the thickest part of the fish. Remove the knife and quickly (carefully) press it to your lower lip. If it is very warm the fish is cooked. Slide the cookie sheet under the salmon between the flesh and skin, leaving the skin stuck to the grill. Use another cookie sheet or a big spatula to scoot the fish onto the cookie sheet.

For the green olive sauce, mix together the olives, lemon rind, shallots, parsley, anchovies, and olive oil in a bowl. Season to taste with salt and pepper. Slide the salmon onto a platter and serve with the green olive sauce.

GRILLED SHRIMP WITH ANCHOVY BUTTER
serves 4

My father came to visit me in Israel, where I had been living for a year. He'd just come from the French Riviera, and nothing in Tel Aviv looked or tasted good to him until we ventured into the Arab section of nearby Jaffa, where we had grilled shrimp like these, cooked over grape-vine cuttings, and doused with salty anchovy butter. That one dish made his visit worthwhile. And he did manage to convince me to come back home. I guess that makes two worthwhile things. —— MH

The anchovy butter is so delicious that you'll want lots of shrimp to mop it up with—the more shrimp the better. Get large, meaty shrimp and if you can get them with the head on, they'll have more flavor. Grilling shrimp with the shell on protects the flesh from drying during cooking.

4 tablespoons butter

16–20 anchovy fillets packed in oil, chopped

2 pounds large shrimp in the shell

1 lemon, halved

Melt the butter with the anchovies in a small saucepan over medium heat. Add a little of the oil from the anchovy jar or tin. Stir occasionally to help the anchovies dissolve into the butter.

Grill the shrimp over a very hot charcoal fire or on a hot gas grill until slightly charred on each side and just cooked through, 2–3 minutes total, depending on the size of the shrimp.

Transfer the shrimp to a serving platter and pour the anchovy butter over them. Serve with a hunk of lemon. Squeeze it over the shrimp. It helps cut the wonderful rich buttery saltiness.

IF IT TASTES LIKE CHICKEN. . .

POACHED CHICKEN EN GELÉE
serves 6

We figured out that Chicken en Gelée is much easier to serve scooped from a shallow bowl rather than slicing the traditional terrine (it all falls apart). Tender chicken, pretty green leeks, and tarragon are all suspended in the clear gelée—a beautiful summer dish with a big wow factor. It is not the least bit complicated. You just have to plan and make it ahead so that it has time to become a gelée.

1 large chicken, cut into pieces
2 carrots, peeled and chopped
2 stalks celery, chopped
1 yellow onion, chopped
Black peppercorns
1 bottle good white wine

3 leeks, well trimmed, washed and sliced into rings
1 envelope unflavored gelatin
Salt and pepper
1 cup tarragon leaves

Put the chicken, carrots, celery, onions, peppercorns, wine, and 3 cups water in a large pot. Add more water if you need to as the chicken and vegetables should be covered. Put the chicken breasts on top as you will be removing them first. Bring to a boil over medium-high heat. Reduce heat to medium-low and cook at a gentle simmer (barely bubbling). Skim off any foam that rises to the surface. Remove the breasts after 30 minutes and set aside to cool. After 1 hour remove the rest of the chicken pieces. When the chicken is cool enough to handle, remove the meat from the bones. Discard the bones. Tear/shred/cut the chicken into large bite-size pieces.

Strain the broth, rinse out the pot, then return the broth to the pot. Add the leeks and simmer over medium-low heat until they are tender, about 30 minutes. Strain the broth and reserve the leeks. Soften the gelatin in 2 tablespoons cold water until it swells, about 5 minutes. Stir the gelatin into the hot broth until it has dissolved. Taste the broth and season with salt and pepper. Add the tarragon to the broth.

Arrange the chicken and the leeks in a large shallow bowl or a deep platter. Pour the broth over the chicken. Make sure the tarragon is evenly distributed. Cover with plastic wrap (not touching the surface of the broth) and refrigerate until the gelée has set, about 3 hours. Serve cold with homemade mayonnaise (page 62), if you like.

TERIYAKI ROAST CHICKEN
serves 4

There are only a few things in life that are really helpful to know, and one of them is that you should always cut the back out of a chicken before you roast it. It makes for much easier carving. And another, is how to make this sweet, sticky teriyaki sauce. This recipe makes 1½ cups so use it on fish, beef, and pork, too.

FOR THE TERIYAKI SAUCE
1 cup brown sugar
1 cup shoyu, or reduced
    sodium soy sauce
1 cup mirin

½ cup chopped peeled fresh ginger
1 tablespoon freshly ground coriander
6 black peppercorns
One 3-pound chicken
Salt and pepper

For the teriyaki sauce, bring the sugar and 1 cup water to a boil in a saucepan over medium-high heat, stirring until the sugar melts. Continue boiling for another minute or two. Reduce the heat to medium and add shoyu, mirin, ginger, coriander, and peppercorns. Simmer, stirring occasionally, until the sauce thickens slightly and has reduced by half, about 1 hour. Strain and store in a covered container in the refrigerator. You can make this ahead.

Preheat the oven to 400°. Use poultry shears or a sharp heavy knife to remove the chicken back by cutting along both sides of the backbone. Rinse the chicken, then pat dry with paper towels. Put the chicken in a large roasting pan and season liberally with salt and pepper. Lay the bird flat on a rack in the pan or re-form it into a round natural shape and tie the legs together with kitchen string. Add 1 cup water to the pan beneath the chicken; this will keep the pan juices from drying up and burning.

Put the chicken in the oven and roast for 45 minutes without opening the door and peeking. Reduce the heat to 300°, then brush the bird with the teriyaki sauce every 5 minutes for 15-20 minutes. The bird is done when a instant-read thermometer registers 165° when stuck into the meaty part of the thigh.

Remove the pan from the oven and allow the bird to rest for 15 minutes to collect itself and re-absorb all its tasty juices before you serve it. Brush the bird a few more times with the sauce. Cut up the chicken, arrange on a platter, and brush with pan juices and more teriyaki sauce.

THE FRY QUEEN'S FRIED CHICKEN
serves 4

Our friend and reigning Fry Queen, Julia Lee (page 20), cuts her chicken up into 10 pieces (2 wings, 2 drumsticks, 2 thighs, 4 breast pieces). This keeps them fairly uniform in size so that they cook evenly and, without the risk of burning the outside crust before the chicken is done. She brines the chicken pieces first to keep the meat moist and tender. Rather than use paper towels, Julia drains her fried chicken on a cooling rack, because it keeps the chicken crispier.

1 cup kosher salt, plus more
  for seasoning
½ cup sugar
1 chicken, cut into 10 pieces

Canola oil
1½ cups flour
1 teaspoon baking powder
Pepper

Put 1 cup salt, the sugar and 4 cups cold water in a large bowl and stir until completely dissolved. Put the chicken pieces into the brine, refrigerate and let them soak for 2 hours. Drain, rinse, and pat the chicken pieces dry with paper towels.

Pour enough oil into a large cast-iron skillet to reach a depth of 2 inches. Heat the oil over medium heat until it registers 350° on a candy thermometer, or use the Chopstick Test (page 21). Meanwhile, whisk together the flour, baking powder, and ½ teaspoon both salt and pepper in a large bowl. Dredge the chicken in the seasoned flour one piece at a time, making sure each piece is well coated. For an extra crunchy coating, Julia likes to double dip the chicken—she dredges and then dredges again about 10 minutes or so later.

Fry the chicken in the hot oil, larger pieces first, skin side down, working in batches if the skillet won't hold all the pieces of chicken at the same time. Turn once, and fry until golden and crispy, about 8 minutes per side. Transfer the fried chicken to a wire rack set over paper towels to drain, and season to taste with salt while still hot.

My friend Kate turned me on to a yummy thing: fried pickles. Sliced dill pickles dipped in buttermilk and dredged in cornmeal. — *Julia Lee*

Hog

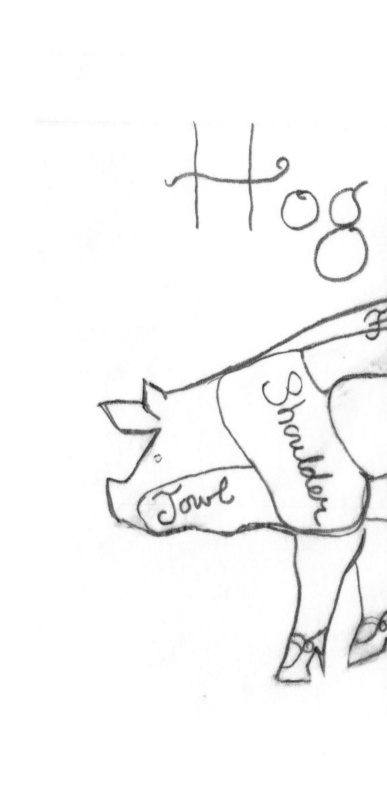

Heaven

Back

in Chops

bs

acon

Ham

CANDIED BACON
makes about 12 pieces

Salty. Sweet. Fat. Crisp. And completely addictive. We first tasted this hors d'oeuvre years ago at a cocktail party in New York City catered by Swifty's, the swanky Upper East Side joint. Serving these is one way to keep guests from hogging the shrimp bowl.

One 8-12-ounce package sliced bacon
1½ cups light brown sugar
Vegetable oil

Preheat the oven to 425°. Separate the bacon strips and blot them dry with paper towels. Spread the brown sugar out in a wide flat dish. Coat both sides of the bacon with the sugar, firmly pressing the sugar onto each strip.

Lay the bacon strips out on a large foil-lined baking sheet (some of the sugar will fall off, but that's okay). Cook the bacon in the oven, turning once, until it is browned and lacquered, 15–20 minutes.

Transfer the bacon strips to a lightly oiled baking sheet to cool. Break in half or into thirds to serve.

HOI-SINFUL SPARERIBS
serves 4

If you can't babysit the ribs on the grill, then cook them in the oven and finish them on the grill to add a little smoky perfume. Even though baby back or county-style ribs look meatier, we prefer spareribs for succulent pork that is finger-lickin' lip-smackin' good.

FOR THE HOI-SINFUL SAUCE	2 cloves garlic, smashed
2 cups hoisin sauce	6 pounds pork spareribs
¾ cup bourbon	Salt and pepper

For the hoi-sinful sauce, mix the hoisin sauce, bourbon, and garlic together in a bowl. Set aside and allow the garlic to flavor the sauce for about 1 hour. Fish out the garlic cloves and discard.

Remove the membrane on the underside of the ribs by loosening it first with a knife on one edge then by pulling it off diagonally with a pair of pliers. It may come off in pieces, that's fine. (Or ask your butcher to do this for you.) Rub the ribs with lots of salt and pepper and then paint all over with some of the Hoi-sinful Sauce. Marinate in the refrigerator overnight.

Preheat the oven to 275°. Put the ribs on a large baking sheet and cook until the meat is tender when pierced with a knife, 2–3 hours. Brush more sauce on the ribs every now and then.

For finishing the ribs in the oven, continue to cook them for another 30 minutes, brushing the ribs with the sauce every 5 minutes. The ribs will develop a "lacquered" glaze.

For finishing the ribs on the grill, preheat a grill. If you are using a charcoal grill, build a small charcoal fire to one side. If using a gas grill, fire up the "back burner" to a medium heat. You want heat and smoke but not direct flame that can cause the sugary glaze on the ribs to burn. Put the ribs on the grill away from and off of the "fire". Cover with the lid and stay near to the grill to manage any flare-ups and to brush the ribs with the sauce every 10 minutes. Cook for 30 minutes.

Remove from the oven or grill and allow to rest for 15 minutes, then cut the slabs into ribs and serve.

PORK LOIN COOKED IN MILK
serves 4

We went on a tear over this recipe. You see it often but it never really works when you make it. After eight tries we figured it out and it was worth it! Serve it hot or cold, as you would vitello tonnato.

One 2-pound boned and tied pork sirloin loin roast or loin end roast

Salt and pepper

2 tablespoons extra-virgin olive oil

2 tablespoons butter

3 bay leaves

2–3 cloves garlic

Zest of one small lemon, in a long ribbon or several large pieces

1 quart whole milk, preferably unhomogenized

Preheat the oven to 300°. Generously season the roast all over with salt and pepper. Heat the oil in a heavy enameled cast-iron pot with a lid over medium–high heat. Brown the roast on all sides. Lower the heat to medium and add the butter, bay leaves, garlic, lemon zest, and milk. Bring the milk just to a boil. Partially cover the pot with the lid, and transfer it to the oven. Cook until the internal temperature of the roast reaches 145°–150° (use an instant-read thermometer), 45–60 minutes.

Remove the pot from the oven. Remove the roast from the pot. Set the meat on a cutting board and cover loosely with foil. On top of the stove, with the lid set on the pot about three-quarters of the way, simmer the milk over medium-low heat until it has reduced by half and soft curds of milk have formed, 60–90 minutes.

Strain the milk through a fine mesh strainer into a bowl. Use a rubber spatula to push the milky solids through the mesh. Whisk until the sauce is smooth. Or for a smoother sauce, purée in a food processor or blender.

Remove and discard the strings from the roast. Thinly slice the meat. Arrange the meat on a platter, spooning a little of the sauce on each slice before layering the next. Spoon remaining sauce on and around the meat. Serve warm, at room temperature, or chilled.

TWO STEAKS FEED FOUR

TWO STEAKS FEED FOUR
serves 4

A thick-cut ribeye, on the bone, is the steak we like for grilling. The bone gives flavor and ballast; the thickness means you can put a good charry crust on the exterior before the interior becomes overcooked. Slather this steak with Parsleyed Butter (page 84) just after you pull it off the grill, or serve it with Green Sauce (page 85) to be spooned on top at the table.

Two 2–3-inch thick, on the bone, ribeye steaks
Salt and pepper

Prepare a hot charcoal or gas grill. Meanwhile, tie each steak to its bone with kitchen string to make a nice neat package so that the meat cooks evenly and doesn't pull away from the bone. Generously season both sides of the steaks with salt and pepper.

Grill the steaks over the hottest section of coals until a good browned crust has developed on the first side, about 8 minutes. To ensure a good crust, resist the urge to move or fiddle with the steaks while they are cooking, but if flare-ups threaten to burn the meat, you've got to move it to a cooler spot on the grill. Turn the steaks and grill the second side for 5 minutes.

Move the steaks to a cooler spot on the grill to finish cooking them, turning occasionally, until the internal temperatures reach 120° for rare, 130° for medium-rare, and 140° for medium, 5–15 minutes longer depending on the thickness of the steaks and the desired doneness.

Pull the steaks off the grill and let them rest for 10–15 minutes. Cut the steak from the bone and slice the meat. Serve both the bones and the meat—you will be fighting over the bones!

Overleaf: Joe and Emil Maresca at their Seargentsville, New Jersey butcher shop, Maresca & Sons.

PARSLEYED BUTTER
makes about ½ cup

Butter seasoned like this used to be called "escargot butter" and we typically slather it on grilled steak, hamburgers, chicken, fish, and poached vegetables, and broil mussels on the half shell with it. We're devoted to Kerrygold salted Irish butter. It's supple, rich, and salty.

8 tablespoons softened butter, preferably salted Irish or other high-fat European-style butter

1–2 cloves garlic, minced

1 shallot, minced

Half a bunch parsley, leaves chopped

Salt and pepper

Beat the butter in a bowl with a wooden spoon to make it smooth and a bit creamy. Add the garlic, shallots, and parsley, and season with salt and pepper. Stir to combine. The butter can be used right away, or covered and refrigerated for up to 3 days or frozen for up to 1 month.

When a recipe calls for minced garlic, we add a little salt to add "grit" to help us mince, right. For a smoother, more subtle garlic flavor, we continue to mince the garlic into a fine paste, left.

GREEN SAUCE
makes about 1 cup

We've taken liberties here and embellished the classic piquant Italian green sauce, salsa verde, with cornichons and preserved lemons. It's a bit of an all-purpose sauce—delicious spooned over roasted, braised, or grilled meats as well as fish and vegetables (especially braised leeks and celery), and great dabbed on hard-boiled eggs (page 14). Make this sauce shortly before using, as it loses its fresh bright flavor if it sits longer than a few hours. Adding the vinegar or lemon juice at the last minute keeps the herbs from turning a dull green.

Half a bunch parsley, leaves chopped
4 sprigs tarragon, chopped
3 scallions, chopped
3 cornichons, chopped
1 tablespoon capers
3 anchovy fillets, chopped

1 clove garlic, minced
Rind of half a preserved lemon
  (page 120), chopped
¾ cup really good extra-virgin olive oil
2 tablespoons fresh lemon juice or
  white wine vinegar
Salt and pepper

Put the parsley, tarragon, scallions, cornichons, capers, anchovies, garlic, preserved lemons, olive oil, and lemon juice into a bowl and stir well. It may well be salty enough so taste the sauce first then season it with salt and pepper. Adjust the flavors with a little more vinegar or lemon juice if you want a brighter, sharper flavored sauce, or with more olive oil if you want it milder.

FIRST YOU BUILD A FIRE

CANAL HOUSE PAELLA
serves 20

Cook something big and involved, something that lures you out of the ordinary, away from the domestic environment of your home kitchen with its tame stove, oven, pots and pans—like this paella. The payoff is exquisitely delicious.

I cup olive oil

I or 2 chickens, cut into even-size pieces (2"–3" is a good size)

I–2 pounds sliced Spanish chorizo

4–6 red bell peppers, cored, seeded, and sliced into fat strips

Lots of chopped parsley

2 onions, chopped

I–2 cloves garlic, chopped

3 tablespoons pimentón

9 cups Valencia, Calasparra, or Bomba rice

2 big pinches toasted saffron threads

9 quarts hot chicken or seafood broth

Salt

3–4 pounds debearded mussels

2 pounds peeled shrimp

Build a fire in a fire pit or in your grill using hardwood, or hardwood charcoal. If cooking in a fire pit, position 4 cinder blocks around the fire close enough to each other to be able set the paella pan on the edge of the blocks above the hot coals. You can also set a sturdy metal grate on top of the cider blocks above the fire. If using a grill, make sure your paella pan fits comfortably on top.

While the fire is burning down, prepare the paella ingredients. The most important ingredient is rice. Figure ½ cup of rice per person. You'll need hot liquid to cook the rice—we like chicken or seafood broth or a combination of broth and water. But the Spanish just use water. For every 1 cup of rice you'll need about 4 cups of liquid. Saffron is essential and toasting the threads for a minute in a hot skillet brings out its distinctive flavor. What and how much else you add to your paella is your choice. The Spaniards tend not to load theirs up. It's more about the rice. Nevertheless, we are red-blooded American "girls" so we pile it on.

When the fire has burned down to a good bed of red-hot coals, rake them out just wide enough to fit under the paella pan. Add some logs or charcoal to the perimeter of the fire. You may need added heat as the paella cooks and the wood or charcoal will be ready to rake into the existing coals by the time you need it later on. You want even, consistent heat under the whole pan.

Set the paella pan over the hot coals. Add the olive oil—use enough to thinly coat the entire surface. Add chicken, turning the pieces as they brown with

a long-handled spoon. Add chorizo, red peppers, and parsley. When the peppers have softened, add onions, garlic, and pimentón and cook, stirring often, until the onions begin to brown. Stir in the rice. Next, crush the saffron threads between your fingers and add it to the hot broth. Generously season the broth with salt. Add about three-quarters of the broth to the pan. Make sure everything is well distributed in the pan. Scatter the shellfish over the rice.

Cook the paella, rotating the pan for even cooking, and do not stir it again. You want the rice to develop a nice deep brown (not burned!) crust on the bottom of the pan. This crust—*socarrat*—is the prized treat of a properly

cooked paella. Let the paella cook and bubble away, raking the coals around to maintain an even heat under the pan. Cook until the rice is tender and the mussels have opened (discard any shells that don't open). Pour more broth over the paella as it cooks if the liquid evaporates before the rice is tender.

Once the rice is tender, let the paella continue to cook a bit longer, allowing the rice to absorb all the liquid. When a brown crust has formed on the bottom of the pan (take a peek) and the edges of the paella begin to dry out and get crusty, the paella is done. The rice takes about 30 minutes to cook.

Remove the paella from the fire and cover it with large clean dishcloths for 15 minutes or so before serving.

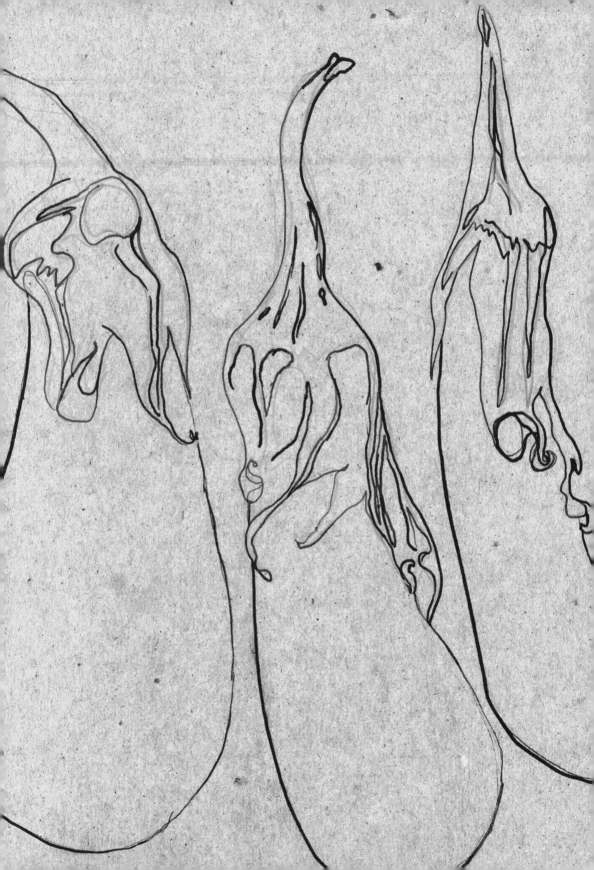

EAT YOUR VEGETABLES

ROASTED EGGPLANT AND ZUCCHINI WITH BREADCRUMBS
serves 6

Roasting these mild vegetables deepens and concentrates their flavors. The bread crumbs absorb the roasting juices and add a nice crunch to the tender vegetables. This recipe is a simpler (though equally delicious) version of French stuffed vegetables (*petits farcis*) where the vegetables—often bell peppers, tomatoes, and onions—are scooped out and refilled with a bread crumb mixture augmented with cooked rice or sometimes ground meat.

1½ cups fresh bread crumbs
Leaves of 1 small branch thyme
1 clove garlic, minced
2 pinches crushed red pepper flakes

¾ cup extra-virgin olive oil
Salt and pepper
3 small eggplants, halved lengthwise
3 medium zucchini, halved lengthwise

Preheat the oven to 350°. Toss the bread crumbs, thyme, garlic, red pepper flakes, and ¼ cup of the olive oil together in a small bowl. Season with salt and pepper.

Using a paring knife, deeply score the flesh of the eggplant and zucchini. Avoid piercing the outer wall of the vegetables. Drizzle some of the remaining olive oil in a shallow roasting pan and arrange the vegetables side by side in the pan. Drizzle more of the remaining oil over the vegetables and season with salt and pepper. Cover each vegetable with some of the seasoned bread crumbs, gently pressing the crumbs into their scored flesh. Drizzle the remaining olive oil over all and season with salt and pepper.

Roast the vegetables in the oven until they are tender and the bread crumbs are toasted golden brown, 30-45 minutes. Drizzle with a little more olive oil, if you like. Serve these warm or at room temperature.

FRIED GREEN TOMATOES
serves 4–6

Toward the end of summer, well after we've had our fill of juicy ripe red tomatoes, the sun isn't strong enough long enough to ripen what's left hanging on the plants. It's then that we begin to consider eating the fruit in its hard green unripe condition—the "second crop", green and plentiful, there waiting for us to pick. We like their faintly sweet, crisp flavor in pickles and chutneys. But better yet are these fried green tomatoes.

4 slices bacon, coarsely chopped

½ cup flour

½ cup cornmeal

Salt and pepper

2 eggs

2 medium green tomatoes, cored
   and thickly sliced

½ cup olive oil

Fry the bacon in a large skillet over medium heat until crisp, about 5 minutes. Lift the bacon out of the skillet with a slotted spoon or with a fork, and drain it on paper towels. Set the skillet with the rendered bacon fat aside.

Mix together the flour and cornmeal in a wide dish and season with salt and pepper. Beat the eggs in a another dish.

Dip the tomato slices one at a time into the egg, then dredge in the seasoned flour and cornmeal. Set the coated tomatoes aside.

Add the oil to the bacon fat in the skillet and heat over medium-high heat. When the oil is hot, fry the tomatoes (work in batches if the tomatoes are going to crowd the skillet) until golden brown, about 5 minutes per side.

Drain the tomatoes on paper towels and season them with a little salt while still hot. Serve the tomatoes with the crisp bacon scattered on top.

Overleaf: Roasted Zucchini with Breadcrumbs, left; green tomatoes, right

CHANTERELLES
serves 4

Fresh chanterelles are dear to us. We forage for them in our woods in the mid-summer and early fall months after there's been a good rainy spell. The thrill of finding them—their pale orange shapes often obscured by the damp leaves and needles on the dark forest floor—must be a primeval one. It delights us to the core every time.

Chanterelles smell moist and mossy, with hints of apricot. Their texture is meaty, chewy, and tender when cooked, and they taste delicious simply prepared with butter, eggs, cream, or fresh herbs.

When you see fresh chanterelles at the market that are still fragrant and moist, spring for them. Otherwise don't spend your hard-earned money.

I pound fresh chanterelles
3 tablespoons butter
I tablespoon extra-virgin olive oil

I–2 cloves garlic, finely minced (page 84)
Salt and pepper
Half a bunch parsley, leaves chopped

Trim off the woody and dirt-caked stem ends from the mushrooms. Using a damp cloth, wipe off any dried leaves or other debris from the rest of the mushrooms (avoid rinsing mushrooms; it tends to ruin their texture). Slice larger mushrooms in half lengthwise or into quarters, the smaller ones are fine to leave whole.

Heat the butter and oil together in a medium skillet over medium-high heat until the butter foams. Add the garlic and mushrooms and season with salt and pepper. Sauté the mushrooms, stirring occasionally, until they have released their juices and are tender, about 10 minutes. Reduce the heat if the pan juices begin to dry up before the mushrooms are finished cooking. Stir in the parsley and adjust the seasonings.

Serve the chanterelles just like this, in the simplest way. Or, spoon them over buttered crusty toast; or onto a pile of soft-scrambled eggs; or over a small mound of creamy polenta; or stir into cooked pasta. Or, let the mushrooms cool, then store them in an airtight container and freeze. This will help you remember the smell of the summer forest in the dead of winter.

SOFT ZUCCHINI WITH HARISSA, OLIVES, AND FETA
serves 4–6

This recipe was one of the five zucchini dishes that Gabrielle Hamilton, the chef/owner of Prune in New York City (and Melissa's beloved sister) prepared during her "battle" against Iron Chef Bobby Flay on that popular television program. Gabrielle managed to slay Flay in that episode, and you'll see why once you taste this sensuous dish. Harissa, the deep red spicy North African chile paste, was her secret weapon.

¼ teaspoon caraway seeds or a combination of fennel and cumin seeds

1 clove garlic

Salt

Juice of 1 lemon

2 tablespoons harissa paste

6 tablespoons really good extra-virgin olive oil, plus a bit more for drizzling at the end

4 zucchini, sliced into thick rounds

Handful cured olives, a combination of oily and briny ones is nice, pitted

½ cup coarsely crumbled feta

Small handful parsley leaves, chopped

Rind of a quarter of a preserved lemon (page 120), chopped

Toast the caraway seeds in a small heavy skillet over medium heat just until they are fragrant, 1–2 minutes. Put the toasted seeds in a mortar and crush them with the pestle. Add the garlic and a good pinch of salt and crush the mixture into a paste. Stir in the lemon juice, harissa, and oil. Season with salt.

Bring a pot of heavily salted water to a boil. Add the zucchini and cook until very tender and soft but definitely not falling apart, about 5 minutes. Drain well, then put the zucchini into a wide bowl and gently toss with the harrisa vinaigrette while still warm.

Dress the zucchini with the olives, feta, parsley, and preserved lemons, finishing the dish with a good drizzle of olive oil.

SWEET AND SOUR ONIONS
serves 6

We like to use cipollini, little flat Italian onions, when good ones are available in the market. But often they are old and dried out, so we use small white boiling or pearl onions instead.

2 pounds cipollini or
   small white onions
6 tablespoons butter
¾ cup sugar

I bay leaf
I cup white wine vinegar
Salt and pepper
2 cups chicken broth or water

To make the job of peeling the onions easier, blanch them for 1–2 minutes in a medium pot of boiling water over high heat, then drain into a colander. When the onions are just cool enough to handle, peel them (their skins slip off more easily when the onions are still quite warm).

Melt the butter in a large nonreactive skillet over medium-low heat. Add the onions, sugar, bay leaf, and vinegar and season with salt and pepper. Cover and cook, occasionally shaking the skillet over the heat, until the onions have softened, 30 minutes.

Add the broth or water, cover, and cook over medium-low heat until the onions are soft but still hold their shape, about 45 minutes.

Uncover the skillet and cook the onions until the juices in the skillet are syrupy, 5-15 minutes. Serve slightly warm or at room temperature.

SWISS CHARD FLAN
serves 4–6

We found two crisp bunches of young red chard at the farmers' market one day. We had been toying with the idea of making a *tourte au blette* (French chard tart) or a quiche, but by evening it was too hot to fool around with making pastry. Some friends dropped by and soon we had opened a bottle of wine and invited them to stay for dinner. This delicate chard flan, which is really a cousin to both the quiche and the frittata, is what we whipped up.

3 tablespoons extra-virgin olive oil
1 large yellow onion, chopped
1 clove garlic, minced
2 bunches young chard, stems and
   leaves chopped separately

3 eggs
1 cup half-and-half
½ cup heavy cream
Salt and pepper
Grated parmigiano-reggiano

Heat the oil in a large nonstick skillet over medium heat. Add the onions and the garlic and cook, stirring occasionally, until just tender, about 10 minutes. Add the chard stems, cover, and continue cooking for another 10 minutes. Add the chard leaves, cover, and continue cooking until leaves have wilted, about 10 minutes.

While the chard cooks, crack the eggs into a mixing bowl and beat in the half-and-half and cream. When the chard has wilted, season with salt and pepper to taste. Pour the eggs and cream over the chard, reduce the heat to low, cover, and cook until the custard has just set, about 20 minutes. It still may be a little jiggly in the middle.

Preheat the broiler. Sprinkle the cheese over the top of the flan and brown it under the broiler. (Leave the oven door ajar if the handle of your skillet isn't ovenproof.) Serve the flan right from the pan or slide it onto a serving platter. Serve at room temperature.

Or if you like, cook the flan in a pre-heated 375° oven the whole time. It will take about 45 minutes.

BERRIES, PLUMS, PEACHES & ICE CREAM

CLASSIC VANILLA ICE CREAM
makes 1 quart

This really is worth making. First of all it's fun. Whenever you start a fresh batch of ice cream, grown-ups and kids alike start asking, "When is the ice cream going to be ready?" As good as hand-crafted and premium commercial ice creams can be, the taste and texture of just-churned homemade ice cream can't be beat. Try this classic vanilla for the pure pleasure of it, and one or two more flavors for kicks—they are all delicious.

1½ cups heavy cream
1½ cups whole milk
¾ cup sugar

1 vanilla bean, split lengthwise
6 egg yolks
Pinch of salt

Put the cream, milk, and ½ cup of the sugar into a heavy-bottomed saucepan. Scrape the seeds from the vanilla bean into the pan, then add the whole bean. Bring the cream and milk to a simmer over medium heat, stirring gently until the sugar dissolves.

Meanwhile, put the egg yolks, salt, and the remaining ¼ cup of sugar into a medium mixing bowl and whisk together until the yolks are thick and pale yellow.

Gradually ladle about 1 cup of the hot cream into the yolks, whisking constantly. Stir the warm yolk mixture into the hot cream in the saucepan. Reduce the heat to low and cook, stirring constantly, until the custard is thick enough to coat the back of the spoon and registers between 175° and 180° on an instant-read thermometer, 10–15 minutes. Stirring the custard constantly as it cooks and thickens helps prevent it from coming to a boil and curdling.

Strain the custard into a medium bowl and add the vanilla bean. Set the bowl into a larger bowl filled with ice, then stir the custard frequently until it has cooled off. Cover the custard and refrigerate it until completely chilled, about 4 hours (though it can keep in the refrigerator for up to 2 days). Discard the vanilla bean.

Churn the custard in an ice cream maker following the manufacturer's instructions. Scoop the ice cream (it will have the consistency of soft-serve) into a quart container with a lid, cover, and freeze for a couple of hours until it is just firm. If you serve the ice cream after it is frozen solid (it will keep for up to 2 days in the freezer), let it soften slightly before serving.

CASSIS ICE CREAM: Press 1 cup of black currant preserves through a sieve into a bowl, then stir in ½ cup crème de cassis. Follow the directions for making Vanilla Ice Cream, stirring the cassis mixture into the chilled custard just before churning the ice cream.

COFFEE ICE CREAM: Follow the directions for making Vanilla Ice Cream, omitting the vanilla bean. Add ¼ cup ground dark-roast coffee or espresso beans to the cream mixture in the first step. (Don't worry, you'll strain out the coffee grounds after the custard has finished cooking in the fourth step.) Add 1 teaspoon vanilla extract to the chilled custard just before churning the ice cream.

PEPPERMINT–PEPPERMINT CRUNCH ICE CREAM: Follow the directions for making Vanilla Ice Cream, omitting the vanilla bean. Stir 2 tablespoons crème de menthe and ¼ teaspoon mint extract into the chilled custard just before churning. Add ¼ cup finely crushed peppermint candies to the ice cream a few minutes before it finishes churning.

STRAWBERRY ICE CREAM: Follow the directions for making Vanilla Ice Cream. While the custard is chilling, toss 1½ cups sliced strawberries with 1 tablespoon sugar in a small bowl and let macerate for an hour or so. Stir the strawberries and accumulated juices into the chilled custard just before churning the ice cream.

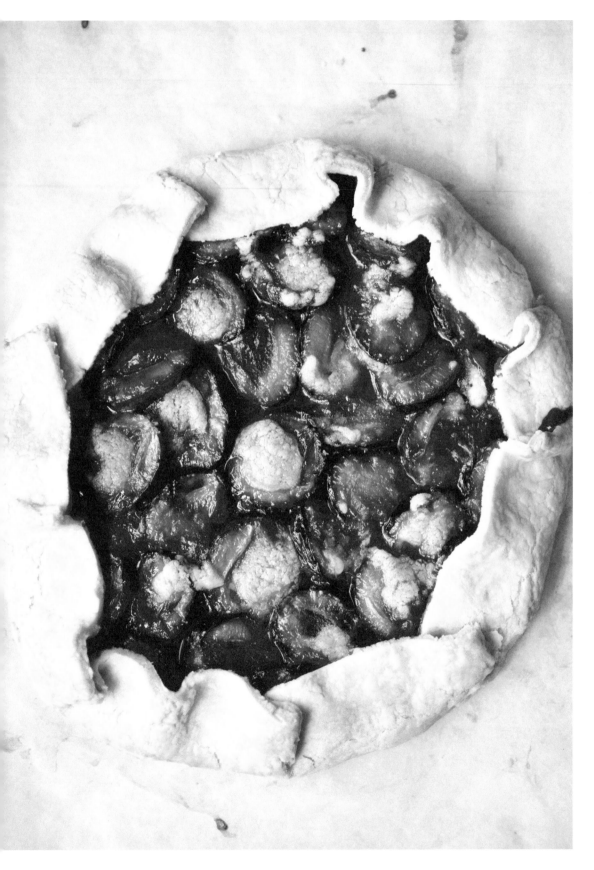

PLUM TART
serves 6

Italian "prune" plums are the perfect variety for making tarts. They are small and meaty, and baking intensifies their flavor. We use frozen store-bought puff pastry and pull it out of the freezer. Then we prepare the plums. By the time we are ready to roll out the pastry, it has defrosted. Baked puff pastry gets soggy after it sits for a while, so make this tart the same day you plan to eat it. If you have some marzipan (or almond paste) on hand, crumble some over the tart when dotting it with butter. —— MH

I sheet (about 10" x 10") puff pastry, defrosted

¼ cup flour

4–6 tablespoons sugar

2 pounds Italian prune plums, halved lengthwise and pitted

4 tablespoons cold butter

2 tablespoons heavy cream

Preheat the oven to 400°. Roll the puff pastry out on a lightly floured surface to a ¼-inch-thick rectangle. Using the tip of a paring knife, lightly score a border about ½ inch from the edge of the pastry. Prick the dough inside the border all over with the tines of a fork to prevent it from puffing up too much during baking. Slide the dough onto a parchment paper–lined baking sheet.

Sprinkle the dough evenly with a few tablespoons of the sugar. Arrange the plums cut side up in the center of the pastry, then sprinkle them with the remaining sugar. Dot the tart with butter and brush the ½-inch border with the heavy cream.

Bake the tart until the pastry is deeply browned around the edges (it's fine—even delicious—if the edges burn a little bit in places) and the plums are soft and jammy and their juices are bubbling and syrupy, 30–40 minutes.

Overleaf: left, Plum Tart; right, Plum Galette

PLUM GALETTE
serves 6

This pastry is a little old-fashioned, but mixing the fats makes a very flaky crust. Don't worry if the edges are a little raggedy—it gives the galette character. Sometimes I use my well-seasoned pizza stone as a baking sheet. I transfer the rolled-out pastry to the cold stone, arrange the fruit on top, and put the stone in the oven. The bottom of the galette is always crisp and golden, never soggy. —— CH

FOR THE PASTRY
1¾ cups all-purpose flour, plus more
   for rolling the dough
1 teaspoon salt
10 tablespoons cold unsalted
   butter, cut into small pieces
2 tablespoons vegetable shortening

5 tablespoons ice water
2 tablespoons heavy cream

FOR THE FRUIT
½ cup sugar
1 tablespoon all-purpose flour
2 pounds Italian prune plums, halved
   lengthwise and pitted

For the pastry, sift together the flour and salt into a large mixing bowl. Add the butter and the shortening and cut them into the flour using a pastry blender, two knives, or even your fingertips. Work the fat into the flour until the mixture resembles very coarse corn meal. Add the ice water tablespoon by tablespoon, sprinkling it over the flour and mixing it in lightly with your hands. Press the mixture together until it forms a mass. Then shape into a flat disc, wrap in plastic, and chill in the refrigerator for about 1 hour.

For the fruit, whisk together the sugar and flour in a large bowl. Add the plums and use your hands to mix them into the sugar until they are well coated. Set aside until you are ready to use them.

Preheat the oven to 375°. Roll out the chilled dough on a floured surface into a 12-14-inch round. Roll the pastry around your rolling pin then unfurl it onto a large baking sheet or a cold pizza stone.

Starting in the middle, arrange the plums on the pastry in a tight circular pattern to about 3 inches from the edge. Fold the edge over the plums, pleating the dough as you go. Brush the pastry with the heavy cream. Bake until the plums are juicy and the pastry golden, 45–55 minutes.

RASPBERRY SANDWICH

When we were little kids, we'd sneak sugar cubes, eating them like candy. When we got a little older, we discovered the delicious combination of buttered bread sprinkled with sugar, and we'd have it for an afternoon snack. All grown up now, we like to embellish the texture and flavor of those childhood sandwiches with the juicy sweetness of fresh raspberries and call it dessert.

Butter a slice of white bread with softened butter (using a full-fat European-style butter like Irish Kerrygold makes all the difference here). Sprinkle sugar over the butter. Scatter fresh raspberries on top and sprinkle with a little more sugar.

Raspberry Sandwich, left; Little Summer Pudding, right

LITTLE SUMMER PUDDINGS
makes 4

This is a quick and easy version of a big summer pudding. We use raspberries, blackberries, tayberries, and boysenberries—but never strawberries or blueberries (it's just our quirky personal preference). Traditionally, this British sweet uses cooked fruit, but we find that ripe summer berries, given a little time to macerate, are plenty juicy—there's no need to cook them.

4 cups fresh raspberries

¼ cup sugar

12 slices white bread, crusts removed

1½ cups milk

1 cup softly whipped cream

Put the raspberries into a bowl and sprinkle the sugar over them. Shake the bowl to mix them together without crushing the berries. Set aside to macerate for a half an hour.

You will need four 6-8–ounce ramekins for your pudding molds. Cut a circle out of each slice of bread, using a ramekin as your template. Pour the milk into a wide dish.

Working with one circle of bread at a time, quickly dip the bread into the milk until just moist but not soggy, then press it into one of the ramekins, lining the bottom. Cover the layer of bread with a generous layer of berries. Make another layer with the moistened bread and berries, then add a third circle of moistened bread. The ramekin should be filled to (even swollen above) the rim. Layer the remaining 3 ramekins in the same fashion using the remaining bread and berries. Spoon any juices over the tops.

Put the filled ramekins on a small tray or into a baking dish, loosely cover each one with plastic wrap or parchment paper, and set a heavy dish directly on top of them as a weight to press the layers together.

Refrigerate the puddings until the bread and berries have completely melded together, about 4 hours. They'll keep well in the fridge for up to 24 hours.

To serve, uncover the ramekins and run a small knife around the inside edges. Invert each pudding onto a dessert plate and unmold it gently. Sprinkle the puddings with some sugar and put a nice spoonful of whipped cream on top.

PEACHES "POACHED" IN WHITE WINE WITH FRESH HERBS
serves 6–8

There are few embellishments worthy of the perfectly ripe in-season peach: some heavy cream and the crunch of a little sugar; a scoop of vanilla ice cream; a warm piece of buttered toast. These complements are just right against the peach's juices and fragrant flesh. So is poaching the fruit in a pretty white wine, infused with sprigs of fresh tarragon or lemon verbena leaves. Choose fully ripe peaches, as their skin will slip off easily when poached. To preserve their delicate flavor and texture, the peaches are best eaten the same day they are prepared.

1 bottle white wine

1 cup sugar

6–8 ripe, in-season peaches

2 branches fresh tarragon or 2 handfuls fresh lemon verbena leaves, or both

Bring the wine, sugar, and 2 cups water to a simmer in a deep medium pot over medium heat, stirring until the sugar dissolves. Carefully add the peaches and blanch them just long enough for their skins to loosen or split, 1–2 minutes. Lift the peaches out of the poaching liquid with a slotted spoon, then slip off their skins. Put the peaches into a deep bowl and cover with plastic wrap, pressing the wrap directly onto the surface to prevent air from darkening the fruit.

Add half of the herbs to the poaching liquid. Let the liquid simmer until it becomes slightly syrupy, about 30 minutes. Set the syrup aside to cool completely. Strain the syrup over the peaches. Add the rest of the herbs, cover with plastic or parchment paper directly on the surface of the peaches and syrup. Let them macerate at room temperature or in the refrigerator for at least 2 hours, and up to 8 hours. Give the fruit a turn to be sure they are "poaching" evenly. Serve the peaches with some of the syrup.

WHY BUY IT IF YOU CAN MAKE IT?

WATERMELON PICKLE
makes about 6 pints

Old pickling recipes often called for slaked lime (calcium hydroxide), which you could buy at corner drug stores. It put the crunch in the pickles—but it isn't readily available anymore. We prefer a more natural ingredient anyway: unrefined sea salt, with its high calcium and magnesium content. Masu Sea Salt from Japan helps keep our pickles crisp. It is one of the few things that we buy through mail order.

I cup unrefined sea salt or
   kosher salt
I medium watermelon, rinsed
   and quartered
5 cups sugar

4 cups white vinegar
2 cinnamon sticks
I tablespoon whole cloves
2 star anise

Dissolve the salt in 8 cups cold water in a large pot. Cut the watermelon flesh from its white-green rind and save the flesh for another use (page 10). Use a knife to remove the green skin, leaving the rind. Cut the rind into 1-inch pieces (you should have 6–8 cups) then add to the salt water, cover, and refrigerate overnight.

The following day, boil the sugar and vinegar together in a medium pot over high heat, stirring often, until the sugar dissolves, 4–5 minutes. Add the cinnamon, cloves, and star anise. Reduce heat to medium, and simmer until reduced by one-third, 25–30 minutes. Meanwhile, drain the rind and cover it with fresh water. Bring to a boil over medium-high heat and boil until translucent, about 15 minutes.

Drain the rinds, return them to the pot, then pour the hot vinegar syrup over them. Reduce heat to low and simmer, stirring often, until the syrup has reduced again by one-third, about 2 hours. Discard cinnamon sticks, star anise, and as many of the cloves as you have the patience to fish out.

Fill a canning pot halfway with water and bring to a boil over medium-high heat. Fill 5–6 hot sterilized pint jars with the hot pickles and syrup, leaving ¼-inch headspace. Wipe the lip of each jar with a damp paper towel, then screw on the hot sterilized lids. Load the jars into the canning pot's rack. Lower the rack into the pot, making sure the water covers the jars by at least 1 inch. Process for 20 minutes. Lift the rack out of the water and set aside, undisturbed, until the jars have cooled completely. Refrigerate after opening.

Overleaf: Making watermelon pickles

LI'S SICHUAN PEPPER AND GINGER PICKLES
makes 2 quarts

Li-fan Huang has a nearby garden nursery where she grows and sells her flowers, herbs, and vegetables. She grew up in Taiwan and came to New Jersey twenty years ago. One day last summer, when we were buying more chives for our window boxes, she ran into her house and came back with a cold jar of these fresh pickles. The taste of them, she said, reminded her of home. We liked their peppery flavor so much that we wrote up her recipe and printed copies for her to share with other customers. We always have a jar or two in the Canal House refrigerator.

16 Asian cucumbers (each about 6 inches long), washed and sliced into ½-inch-thick rounds

¼ cup kosher salt

3 tablespoons vegetable oil

3 large pinches Sichuan peppercorns

5 cloves garlic, thinly sliced

2 fat fingers of fresh ginger, peeled and thinly sliced

¼ cup sugar

1½ cups rice wine vinegar

Put the cucumber slices in a large bowl, sprinkle with the salt, mix well, and set aside.

Heat the oil over medium heat in a large skillet. Add the peppercorns and sauté for about 3 minutes to release their flavor. (Li advises that if you like a less spicy pickle, remove and discard about three-quarters of the peppercorns at this point). Add the garlic and ginger, and sauté for about 3 minutes. Add the sugar and rice wine vinegar and bring to a simmer, stirring occasionally, until the sugar melts.

Drain the cucumbers of any liquid (leaving the salt on) then pour the hot vinegar, along with the garlic, ginger, and peppercorns, over the cucumbers and toss well. Transfer to two quart containers with tight-fitting lids. Refrigerate for a couple of days, turning at least twice a day to give everything a chance to marinate. The pickles are now ready to eat. They will keep for about 2 weeks in the refrigerator.

PRESERVING LEMONS

Counterclockwise from top left: A small batch of just-made preserved lemons; packing salt into an almost quartered lemon; Meyer lemons; two jars of preserved lemons. The one on the left has just been prepared and the one on the right has been curing for two months. See recipe on page 120.

PRESERVED LEMONS

Everyone needs a few culinary tricks up their sleeve—or, better yet, in their refrigerator. If you live in a metropolitan area with lots of ethnic shops, you'll be able to find these lemons already cured. Living far from those stores, we make our own—big jars of them that last us throughout the year. And it is so well worth it. These golden treasures are money in the bank as their deep salty-sour flavor can brighten up practically any dish. Actually, we have to restrain ourselves from using them in just about everything.

We like to use Meyer lemons, a sweet, thin-skinned variety (most likely a cross between a mandarin orange and a true lemon). You'll find them in the market from fall through spring. But any variety of lemon will do. In fact, a thicker-skinned lemon is the traditional choice in Morocco, where this pickling method originated.

Preserved lemons are typically rinsed before they are added to stews, tagines, soups, and couscous dishes. Only the rind is used and the pulpy flesh gets discarded. When our own preserved lemons are still new (aged between one month and about six months), we use both rind and flesh, not even bothering to rinse the lemons. The salty brine softens the rind until it is almost translucent and makes the flesh plump and supple. The longer the lemons cure, the saltier they get, so taste them first to decide how you will cook with them. Preserved lemons will last up to 1 year in the fridge.

Lemons, washed
Kosher salt
Sterilized wide-mouth container with a tight-fitting lid

Cut the lemons (almost all the way through) into quarters, keeping them attached at the stem end. Working over a bowl, tamp the inside of each lemon with salt. Tightly pack the salt-filled lemons into the sterilized container. Pour more salt over the lemons as you fill the container. Cover the salt-packed lemons with freshly squeezed lemon juice.

Store in the refrigerator. Turn the container occasionally for the first few weeks to moisten all the lemons with the ever-accumulating salty brine. The lemons should eventually become submerged in this brine. If the brine doesn't completely cover them after a month, use a metal kitchen spoon to gently press the lemons under the surface.

BREAD CRUMBS
makes 4 cups

We have a thing for freshly made bread crumbs. In fact, our freezer is packed with bags and plastic containers of them. When we're in a hurry or when we have a lot of day-old bread, we embrace technology and use the food processor to make quick work of them. When the bread is a little dried out, we grate it on the large holes of a box grater. And when there is enough time and the bread is fresh, we cut off the crusts in big wide pieces and tear the crumb with our fingers into uneven shapes as coarse or fine as we want the way Christopher's grandmother taught her to do. (Their jagged edges make for better crunch when they're toasted.)

We like the frugality of making crumbs from unused bread. But more than that, we like how toasted bread crumbs add texture and body to almost everything—soups, pastas, roasted vegetables or fruits, fish, meats, even desserts. For the most evenly browned bread crumbs, we toast them in the oven, though small batches can quickly be browned in a skillet on top of the stove.

4 tablespoons butter

2 tablespoons extra-virgin olive oil

4 cups fresh bread crumbs

Salt

Preheat the oven to 350°. Melt the butter and the olive oil in a small pan over medium heat. Put the bread crumbs into a large bowl and pour the butter and oil over them. Season with salt and mix together until the bread crumbs are well coated. Spread the bread crumbs evenly in a large baking pan. Toast in the oven, stirring occasionally, until the bread crumbs are crisp and evenly colored a deep golden brown, 10–15 minutes.

Use the bread crumbs or transfer the cooled crumbs to a container with a tight fitting lid. They'll keep a few days at room temperature or in the freezer for up to month.

Christopher Hirsheimer and Melissa Hamilton in the Canal House kitchen

CHRISTOPHER HIRSHEIMER served as food and design editor for *Metropolitan Home* magazine, and was one of the founders of *Saveur* magazine, where she was executive editor. Christopher has cowritten four cookbooks, the award-winning *Saveur Cooks* series and *The San Francisco Ferry Plaza Farmers' Market Cookbook*. She is a writer and a photographer. Her pictures have illustrated more than thirty cookbooks for such notables as Julia Child, Jacques Pépin, Lidia Bastianich, Mario Batali, Rick Bayless, and Frank Stitt. Her photographs have also appeared in such magazines as *Saveur*, *Instyle*, *Food & Wine*, *Country Home*, *Metropolitan Home*, and *Town and Country*.

MELISSA HAMILTON cofounded the restaurant Hamilton's Grill Room in Lambert-ville, New Jersey, where she served as executive chef. Following her tenure there, she embarked on a career in food styling, and recipe testing and development for cookbooks and food magazines. This included stints at *Martha Stewart Living* and *Cook's Illustrated*. Melissa joined *Saveur* first as director of the test kitchen, and then became food editor. Her styling work has appeared in numerous cookbooks for such well-known chefs as David Tanis, Joyce Goldstein, Roberto Santibañez, and Michael Psilakis.

Christopher and Melissa opened their own studio, Canal House, in 2007. They now self-publish *Canal House Cooking* and continue to collaborate, photographing and designing cookbooks.